THE
SCHOOL
OF THE
SPIRIT

THE SCHOOL OF THE SPIRIT

Beryl R Moore

Sovereign Ministries

Published by Sovereign Ministries

ISBN number: 978-1908-154-354

Cover design by Esther Kotecha, EK Designs (add normal text)

Typeset by Avocet Typeset, Somerton, Somerset, TA11 6RT

Printed in the UK

DEDICATION

I dedicate this book to Holy Spirit,
whose inspiration and oversight
made it possible

'Shoreless Ocean! Who shall sound Thee?
Thine own eternity is round Thee, Majesty Divine!'

Frederick William Faber

TABLE OF CONTENTS

Contents

ACKNOWLEDGEMENTS

I acknowledge the debt I owe to other writers and the people without whom this book would never have been conceived.

Women such as Julian of Norwich, Teresa of Avila, Catherine of Sienna, and Madam Guyon, who opened my eyes to the reality of the 'School of the Spirit'.

The mighty men of God: Andrew Murray, T. Austin Sparks, A. W. Tozer, Derek Prince, and Roger Price, all of whom have gone to their reward.

In the past twenty years, singularly the influence and instruction of Graham Cooke, has transformed the way I think and perceive the things of the Spirit. What a man! Thank you Graham, look forward to seeing you when we get there!

My gratitude would not be complete without mentioning the work of my Trustees over the past 25 years, who have so faithfully steered the ministry under the guidance of the Holy Spirit.

Last but by no means least, my thanks to Sue Corbett, Carol Demuth and Deborah Preddie who have sacrificially given time to proof read, check copyrights and do all the hundred and one other things required to bring a book into print.

Beryl R Moore

Thanks girls. I salute you all.

God bless you.

Beryl Moore

WHAT OTHERS SAY ABOUT BERYL MOORE

I have known Beryl Moore for many years and can testify to the fact that this is a not a book of theoretical principles but a route map for the journey that Beryl herself has taken into the heart of God.

If you like your devotional to leave you feeling as though you have been wrapped in a warm, fluffy blanket then this devotional is not for you!

But if you want 'more,' desire to 'go deeper' and long to 'climb the mountain' with Jesus, then this will be your map, guide and handbook for the journey.

This is a devotional that challenges and inspires you to get out your spiritual armour, buff it up and re-clothe yourself, to take up your sword and shield and put your helmet firmly on. It is a call to discipleship not a comfort blanket.

This series will confront you and make you uncomfortable – it is a School of the Spirit that will leave you changed – as changed as you choose to be.

This book is a challenge to choose the crucified life and to choose to be 'determined to know nothing among you except Jesus Christ, and Him crucified.'

If the desire of your heart is to be a watchman on the wall, a dweller in the secret place, to be found with oil in your lamp when the Bridegroom returns and to 'live your life before an audience of One' then welcome to the journey of a lifetime...

Jennifer Rees Larcombe
Author and Founder of Beauty from Ashes

The School of the Spirit is a gem. It is both inspired and revelatory; a book you will want to reread and ponder again. For those who long to understand what it means to live in the Spirit, it will journey you into the very heart of God; it will irresistibly draw you into deeper dimensions of his love. Written with unique style and delightful humour, it will open your eyes to the wondrous possibilities of living in intimate union with Jesus and ignite a desire for his fullness. Embracing its profound truths and wisdom will leave you transformed.

Greta Peters
Co-Director, SpiritLife Ministries

Beryl Moore is a lady who spends her days in a country cottage, reading God's word, praying and encouraging others in the way of faith. She calls you 'dear' and treats you like family when you visit, but she never hides the truth. She quotes James Bond, Mr. Beaver, and sings songs, but her message is earnestly sharp. She sits by the fireside knitting and simultaneously uses social media, podcasts and videos. To many she is 'a legend,' to some a spiritual mother, to most

12

she is a wise friend who is always there for you. She respects your privacy and never forces her opinion, but when you ask for it, boy she gives it! Her legacy is being built as a humble contented lady who knows she is also a general in God's kingdom. Saints like Beryl Moore are few and far between, and we are all blessed to know her. In this easily readable and powerful little book Beryl asks if you are ready, "To begin your life again, this time living from the inside, out....to enrol in the School of the Spirit?" Stick with the programme if you answered in the affirmative! And hold on to your hat! Nothing is going to be the same again, but it's brilliant! Transformation guaranteed!!

Pete Stanley
Director of Ment4

Never has so much been conveyed in such few words... each teaching is a pearl of wisdom that comes straight from the throne room of God that leaves you feeling challenged, convicted, inspired and loved.

Rev Paul Unsworth
Founder and Pastor of Kahaila

I've gotten to know Beryl well over the past three years and she is really a mentor like no other! Her heart for growing and equipping the Church is shown through the way she teaches, no matter if the teaching is to one person or a hundred, online or otherwise. The School of the Spirit is not just a handy manual or nice little collection of devotionals. It is to challenge and start changing our thinking to a kingdom perspective. Certainly a game-changer!

Greg Corbett
Worship Leader and Songwriter

FOREWORD

Meeting Beryl is an experience in its own right. It is a joyful confrontation! It has been many years since I first met Beryl and still clearly remember the warm welcoming and genuine smile which left me thinking I had known her forever. She is full of words many of them from the Scriptures. As you listen you sense God's wisdom and you realise there is much more to Beryl. We may have our own thoughts about positive confession of Scripture but I know this precious woman has proved so much in this area.

She is a survivor and certainly not a victim. She too has experienced the difficult issues of life as well as the many blessings. Does Beryl stay down when knocked down? Not likely, she's up and will carry on trusting her Saviour to lead her well. She is an overcomer and a fighter yet is sensitive to the Holy Spirit in hearing and obeying, as well as being honest, openhearted, and transparent and without guile.

What you see is what you get and this core area of her personality has been fashioned through many decades. She has dug deep in her search and study of the Scriptures over the years and found many hidden treasures. They are the secret riches that our Heavenly Father has hidden for us to find if we are willing to search too. In other words, keep listening and you'll pick up the gems that come out of the experience and revelation of her personal walk with the Lord.

The School of the Spirit is an amalgam of experience, anecdotes, and revelation from Beryl's life and beloved Scripture. As you read this devotional, you enter into a faithful woman's life, full of heart and passion for the Kingdom of God. Is she a pastor, a teacher, or an evangelist? In all probability all three, but she is most certainly prophetic.

Beryl may have many years behind her yet she has a legacy to leave. Something that will endure and lay foundations for the next generation, as well as reminding us not to miss out, but to get on with all that we are called to do. This devotional is part of that legacy.

It will challenge, confront, and certainly inspire.

I commend it to you…

Rev Steve Hepden MTh
Author of 'Rejection Hurts'

PREFACE

These teachings were originally published on Facebook just prior to Christmas 2016, they then continued for the month of January 2017. It is my prayer and hope you will both enjoy and benefit from them.

This book is more than a devotional; it is a tool to make you think deeply about your life and walk with God through the power of His indwelling Holy Spirit.

During the course of your time with Him, the Holy Spirit will change you, if you let Him.

As you enter His school you will find you are in just that, school; that His ways are not yours (or even the ways of your church). You may find you need to make some radical mid-course corrections in your thinking because life in the Spirit is about displacement, and there may be major adjustments in your theology as He presents Himself as He really, really is, not as you think He is.

To get the most from this book then, there is an urgent need that you slow down, learn to be still and to think deeply about your relationship with God; with yourself; and with those around you. The Fall separated us in all three areas, not just one… from God, from ourselves and from our fellow man.

Peace and stillness are in short supply, but if you will practise bringing yourself to a place of stillness for just ten minutes a day – it's just a discipline you can do this thing – the quality of your life and therefore your effectiveness in the Kingdom will increase exponentially.

As you allow the indwelling Holy Spirit to bring you back to your centre, your God consciousness will rise and you will find that He really is in control of all things.

God is restoring the Creator/creature relationship. Ours is to sit in wonder at His feet, gazing on the crucified; knowing that our lives are hid with Christ in God and He has everything covered… I encourage you to think deeply about these messages and as you practise the art of being still, you will desire more and more of the Person you meet in that place of stillness and you will discover that the Kingdom really is, within you.

Come to this journal then with an open mind and a heart prepared to bow before Him in adoration and worship, I guarantee you will never be the same again.

God bless you.

Beryl

1 War And Peace

We give Him in a time of peace what He extracts from us in a time of war.

When I hadn't long been saved, I was luxuriating in His presence and in a moment of total abandonment I said, "Whatever you ask I will do".

Seconds later I heard His voice.

"I want you to give up smoking..."

At this time, newly saved, I was still smoking more than 40 cigarettes a day...

My first reaction was, "I can't do it!"

But He showed me what He required and how I could, in His strength, do this thing.

I was to pray in tongues every time I wanted a cigarette.

I have never had one from that day to this.

What is He asking for today that you gave Him in a moment of abandonment?

You can be sure He will come right in behind to give you the ability and the power to do it and you will never look back.

God bless you as you continue in the School of the Spirit on His Majesty's Service.

2 His Thoughts Are Not Our Thoughts

Jesus' mother Mary is at the wedding in Cana.

They are running out of wine.

Mary quietly urges Him to do something about it.

But He considers it ahead of time saying in effect, "Mum you're out of sync."

She has got an idea; she knows Jesus is going to start His ministry soon and thinks now would be a good time...but He says, "My time has not yet come."

"Mother dear, the place where I live is different from the place where you live; your thoughts are not my thoughts."

When we embark on this journey in the School of the Spirit we will very quickly find He just doesn't think the way we do!

He doesn't view things the way we do, or do things in the time frame we think He is going to, or indeed should! He seems to delay His coming...and we are apt to say, "Lord, you are late – again".

We have no more idea of His thoughts than the sheep have the mind of the shepherd – as He told me once – I went home and told my cat the same thing; he smiled impassively as cats do...

We are in a different realm, He's saying to Mary. I live from a different place.

He lives from the inside to the outside.

From His spirit not His soul.

From heaven, not earth.

For us we find that in His realm we must die to live, give to receive, and allow Another's will to take precedence over ours, life becomes somewhat problematic.

Living from the Spirit will cause us to make major adjustments because there is another king.

As with Herod when he heard of the birth of Jesus and learnt there was another king, we are disturbed; the king of self must be dethroned, and he doesn't give way without a struggle... now there are two wills at work, the will of the Spirit of God and self-will.

Which one is winning for you right now? Your level of peace will be the litmus test here.

On a scale of 1 – 5 then, 5 being very peaceful, what's your peace level like?

If it's low, you can be sure you are fighting Him somewhere.

Quick answer to that one is a slap on the rear and the command, "Get in line Winifred!!" That's from Jungle Book I think…[1]

Note
1. *The Jungle Book – classic Disney animation based on Rudyard Kipling's book*

3 Comprehension

We looked at Mary's understanding of Jesus, and today I want to look at how the disciples really didn't comprehend where Jesus was coming from either, just like us...

During those three and a half years they learned how 'other than' them, He was, and sometimes the lesson was a hard one.

But they had to learn it.

It was as they lived and travelled with Him they found themselves again and again clashing with His thoughts, His mind, and His ways.

They would urge Him to do things, to go places or take a certain course: they sought to bring to bear on Him their worldview and their judgements.

A classic from Luke is*, "Shall we call down fire?"* and His response, *"You know not what manner of spirit you are of!"* [1]

Even though they lived with Him, they hadn't got a clue.

Looking with their natural eye they wanted to bring judgement on those who wouldn't receive Him...He would have none of it; their best suggestions were utterly useless, their hearts were hard.

All the time He patiently brought them back and showed them: *'My thoughts are not your thoughts, neither are My ways, your ways'.* [2]

Same for us; His ways, His ideas, His judgements are altogether different. They may have said as we do, "Lord, why is it I'm always caught out saying and doing the wrong thing? Why am I always messing up?" To which He replies, "I am teaching you, that's all; I am bringing you to see My ways. When you have learned that you really don't know, then we can begin to build, but until you have learned that first lesson that I am altogether 'other than you,' we can't progress".

So therein lies the first lesson in the School of the Spirit, we **don't** know; we need to be taught.

It is quite reassuring really, to see that for all our knowledge, age and experience we are back in kindergarten with the sweetest Teacher we could wish for.

That is, if pride doesn't get in our way – but that wouldn't apply to you would it now? But just in case it does, may I suggest you pray for a teachable spirit, that's a prayer that always gets an answer…

Notes
1. Luke 9:54-6
2. Isaiah 55:8

4 Education Begins

So we see that Jesus first presents us with Himself, He shows us how lovely He is, and then He begins to produce His nature within us, and this is where our true education begins...

It is in the School of the Spirit that we learn that the mind of man, at its best, is 'other than' the mind of Christ and the Holy Spirit's job is to see to it that we are *'transformed by the renewing of... [our] mind'*,[1] in order that we may love Him with all our heart, soul, mind and strength.

Loving Him and His ways with our mind is a very special thing.

The mind is the powerhouse, *'As a man thinks in his heart, so is he'*,[2] Proverbs tells us...what we think and believe leads to how we live...

In the School of the Spirit we learn to control our thoughts so that they dwell, stay, and remain, fixed on His goodness and kind intention towards us, no matter what is happening around us...We learn to seek Him for Himself, not what He can do for us...

As our love matures, we are emptied of self and filled with Him.

We cease the refrain, "What about me?" and focus on the desires and aims of our Bridegroom lover...

Our world-view changes and we get our information not from the earth, but from heaven.

We become heavenly minded making us a force for good in the earth...

'Jesus went about doing good...'[3]

We begin to stay where we have been put, in Christ; and the things of the earth do grow strangely dim in the light of His glory and grace.

We never recognise our own motives for doing things and thinking things until the Holy Spirit really gets working in us...

Self it appears comes up all the time and we discover our best intentions are defiled and our purest motives are unclean because self is at the root.

That old rebel **self** is revealed in everything we say and do until we say, as Jesus did to Peter, *'Get behind me Satan',*[4] and agree with Paul, *'In me* [in my old self] *dwells no good thing'.*[5]

We come to the place where we have seen and acknowledge

that only the Christ in us is worth listening to...

What a deliverance it is to be free of the old man! Little wonder Paul says, "R*eckon yourselves dead therefore to sin but alive to God in Christ".*[6] Again the blessed Holy Spirit is reinforcing that Jesus is one thing and we are another.

But we are not downhearted, we recognise we are a work in progress; we are saved, we are being saved and we will be saved.

What extraordinarily **GOOD** news that is isn't it? We are not where we were, we are not where we are going to be, but we are on our way!!

Notes

1. Romans 12:2 *renewing of the mind*
2. Proverbs 23:7 ... *as a man/woman thinks, so is he/she.*
3. Acts 10:38 *God anointed Jesus with Spirit of truth & grace*
4. Matthew 16:23 ... *be mindful of the things of God*
5. Romans 7:18 ... *in my flesh dwells no good thing ...*
6. Romans 6:11 ... *dead to sin, but alive to God in Yeshua Messiah, our Boss*

5 Complete In Him

So this is grace indeed, I stand complete in Him.

'Clothed in His righteousness alone,

Faultless to stand before the throne.'[1]

How the realisation of this saves us from dead works! We can't do a thing to make ourselves better!

I cannot change myself or pull myself up to another level; this is my first and most important lesson in the School of the Spirit – I am fatally flawed and if He doesn't effect change in me, I can't do it!

All is grace.

The empowering presence of God in me.

What a Christmas present all over again.

The pressure is off.

'All my efforts are as filthy rags'.[2]

The remedy is easy.

Yield, that's all I have to do, that alone is my part in this transformation process.

Give up, give way, let go...

Yield.

Submit.

Surrender.

Ah.

Didn't He say somewhere, *"My yoke is easy and my burden light...and you will find rest for your souls"*?[3]

In the words of Fanny Crosby:

'Perfect submission, all is at rest,

I in my Saviour am happy and blessed,

Watching and waiting looking above,

Filled with His goodness, lost in His love.' [4]

So, in the light of this, how's it working out for you?

Notes
1. From the Hymn: Edward Mote, *My Hope is Built on Nothing Less*
2. Isaiah 64:6
3. Matthew 11:29-30 NIV
4. From the Hymn: Fanny J Crosby, *Blessed Assurance*

6 An End And A Beginning

What we have, in essence, learned so far is that before we can truly be ready for the School of the Spirit we must come to the end of ourselves.

Until we actually reach that place where we despair of ourselves and recognise He really is totally different from us and unless we start again, we'll never see the fullness of His kingdom in our lives.

There is not one instance where He sees things the way we do, and despair is our companion.

What an excellent place that is to be!

Ask Peter and the other disciples.

They were going to follow Him to hell and back – then He said, *"I'm going to the cross."*

'The hour is coming… [when] you will be scattered.'.[1]

And to one He said, *'You will deny Me'.*[2]

It all happened just as He said it would and they were in despair – catch up with them on the road to Emmaus.

He had to let them come to the end of themselves – so they could begin in Him.

God can't begin until we reach an end.

So having reached rock bottom, His life can begin to be made manifest in us and through us.

He cannot do through us what He hasn't been able to do in us...

It's all good: He's preparing the way, clearing the ground to build something and He does it by emptying us of ourselves.

Two things can't occupy the same space.

'Something's got to give'[3] as the old song goes.

It doesn't feel good particularly, in these days of concern about our self-esteem and self-worth; it's deflating to admit actually *'In me dwells no good thing'* [4] but it's the qualification for life in the Spirit…

Without Him, you can do nothing,* that's all.

of eternal value

The School of the Spirit

If there was anything worth salvaging we wouldn't have needed a new start with a new DNA, He needn't have died, He could have just sent an angel with paint and wallpaper to patch us up...but there was nothing for it but to start all over again...

His ways we see, yet again, are not our ways; they are so much higher; altogether 'other worldly'...

So we have a new start, a new heart, a new life where what we choose empowers or diminishes us according to what we choose, but we'll look at that another time, for the moment we need to assess where we are right now.

How's it working out for you?

Are you empty enough to embark on the journey?

To begin your life again, this time living from the inside, out...

To enrol in the School of the Spirit?

Stick with the programme if you answered in the affirmative! And hold on to your hat! Nothing is going to be the same again, but it's brilliant!

Transformation guaranteed!!

I promise you a crown.

Absolutely certain.

He's said so.

Notes
1. John 16:32 , *Jesus friends scattered alone, but God is with Him*
2. Luke 22:61 *Peter denying Jesus, realizing - weeping bitterly*
3. From the Song: Johnny Mercer, *Something's Gotta Give*
4. Romans 7:18 *trials, sufferings are nothing compared to God's glory and victory over man's inhumanity to man.*

7 Recap

We have seen three things:

1. He is altogether not like us, He is different.

2. Of ourselves we can never be like Him, though that is what He desires.

3. It must be **ALL** Him if we are to change.

Life in the Spirit, therefore, is – different.

'Not what I am Lord, but what Thou art.' [1]

No longer two lives to be lived but one.

'For to me, to live is Christ and to die is gain' [2]

If we can say that and mean it, we are on the same page

as the Holy Spirit and His work of transformation can commence.

We spoke about a crown.

'Henceforth is laid up for me a crown of righteousness'.[3]

Now the Holy Spirit can begin to work in, what was imputed to us at the moment of salvation.

He can begin to show us how to live by the kingdom mandate – the Sermon on the Mount as He empowers us to live righteously and learn the Royal law of love.

Keeping His commandments is not burdensome...

It is only problematic when we resist.

If we resist now, conflict will become a constant companion.

We learn to yield.

To surrender...

All the time...

Not now and again.

Life in the Spirit is not only different; it's about:

Displacement

Discipline

Desire

Delight!

Stick with the programme!

We're getting to the really interesting part…

Notes
1. From the Hymn: Horatius Bonar, *Not what I am, O Lord*
2. Philippians 1:21 NIV
3. 2 Timothy 4:8 KJV

8 Displacement

So life in the Spirit, in the School of the Spirit, is different and it's about displacement.

In displacement we get nothing from a place of rush or hurry...

God is not constantly on the hoof.

He isn't panicked by circumstance.

He's not pressured by situations.

He lives in a place of unbroken delight, peace and joy.

Joining Him here we learn the Secret of the Secret Place –

'Martha, Martha...Mary has chosen the better part'.[1]

Sitting at His feet, we learn to still ourselves and keep on stilling ourselves, shutting out all the things that seek to distract us.

If we don't, we gain nothing.

This is not the place of the quick fix, the 'spiritual shot' to keep you going between crises.

The ups and downs of good and bad meetings...

We are learning a different way of living.

From a different place.

We will no longer be subject to our circumstances...

Our circumstances will be subject to us...

It begins with this 'D' word, displacement.

Displacing our turmoil with His peace.

Accustomed as we are to living from our soul where our happiness depends on what happens, we are learning to live from the deep well Jesus is digging and constantly filling, on the inside of us...from our spirit man.

There we can drink both sparkling and still water...any time we like...

He is the water of Life.

Drinking from Him we will never thirst again.

But the journey to this Secret Place will not be easy.

He makes sure it isn't.

Here the true battle for your soul takes place.

Everything and everyone (bless 'em) will conspire to invade your peace.

He allows it.

To strengthen you.

The devil is there to strengthen you spiritually; people are there to grow in you the fruit of the Spirit.

So everything is for your increase, profit, expansion, multiplication or upgrade.

Cool!

All good.

The whole point is…peace is a weapon...

And your circumstances are how you learn to use that weapon effectively.

They are your training ground where you learn to wage war with your peace.

This is where you learn to keep the peace Jesus has already given you.

'My peace I give you...'[2]

You have it; now you are learning to keep it and use it.

To use it to battle the circumstances and situations in which you find yourselves.

You need trials to practise on...to practise holding your peace...until you have 101lbs pressure on the inside to 100lbs pressure on the outside.

Brilliant, only He would think of that!

You are learning to recover and hold your own inner territory, which was lost at the Fall...

So pressure must come...

You can't be an overcomer without something to overcome – to state the obvious...

It is at this point you will be tempted to cave in, give up, and surrender to the situation and the enemy of your soul because you think it, or he, is stronger.

No, No, No!

This is where you really discover what *'Christ in you, the hope of glory'*[3] really means.

The School of the Spirit

You discover how your choices empower or diminish you, according to which way you choose to go...life in the Spirit is about choices.

Nobody drifts to the top of a mountain...

Notes
1. Luke 10:42
2. John 14:27
3. Colossians 1:27

9 Desire – His Towards You

The third of our 'D' words is desire; difference, displacement, desire.

This is where He conforms you to His desire...

Thomas à Kempis wrote long ago, **'The Lord has many lovers of His crown but few lovers of His cross.'**[1]

His aim is that you will embrace and love the cross, desire it, in exactly the same way as He did.

We ended the last session saying no one drifts to the top of a mountain.

They don't do they, if it's a big one, months of training precede the climb? And you need the right kit, plimsolls won't do for your feet...boot camp...getting that body under control, and the mind too.

Mountain climbing is as much about mental stamina as physical.

No cross no crown.

Who said that?

I'll have the crown, not so sure about the cross bit though...

But if we let the Holy Spirit have His way with us, we find our language begins to change: our prayer life changes from 'gimme, gimme, gimme', to asking for something completely different: we now see that what we need are the three wounds – **'The wound of contrition, the wound of compassion, and the wound of seeking after God...'** [2]

Our focus has shifted from us and our needs, to His agenda, His desire.

The Lord not only desires to save us, but once saved; He then seeks to train us for eternity with Himself.

There is a difference, beloved, between being saved by Him and being trained by Him for our life with Him in eternity.

Salvation is the free gift of grace; it comes to us not by our works or striving but by faith which He gives us.

But, being trained by the Lord is not free.

It comes with a price – it costs us to forgive and it costs us to love, it costs us to deny the self-life and it costs us put aside lesser goals to follow Him.

Salvation is a gift but if we want to be like Him and enrol in the School of the Spirit we must accept the invitation to be 'fully trained' because it is the path to maturity.[3]

So the question comes again, just how much of Him do you really, really, want? Only you can answer that one.

To help you, please keep in mind:

'You are His treasure, a holy nation, His people, the people of His power, the people of His passion, the people of His heart, the people of His affection; you are more glorious than you know, stronger than you look, more brilliant than you can imagine – this is your identity; this is who you are – do not permit anybody to talk you out of it or talk you down from that high place, that high calling. You are in Christ, you are astonishing; and at the very least you are wonderful, His marvellous darling...' [4]

That might help you in your decision making...to know just *HOW* He sees you...

'His desire is towards you'.[7]

Notes
1. A W Tozer *The Voice of the Prophet* Bethany House Publishers USA 2014 Chapter 11
2. A W Tozer *Man-The Dwelling Place of God* Christian

Publications Pennsylvania 1966 p101 (Julian of Norwich)
3. Luke 6:40
4. From the CD The Art of Thinking Brilliantly by Graham Cooke

10 Difference And Displacement, Desire And Discipline

Desire and Discipline

What we have been talking about and what the Spirit is trying to teach us, if you hadn't realised it, is His desire is that we understand, learn and live in the Law of the Kingdom of God.

The Royal Law.

The law of **LOVE**…

This is what our schooling is all about – in a word – learning the discipline of loving.

How, you ask, can loving **be** a discipline?

Simply my darling because again, His love is totally different from ours…it is self-giving, not self-referential. "Not I'll love you if...." or "I'll love you when..." but I love you without any conditions attached right now.

I'll love you if you spit in my eye, if you rob me, cheat on me and steal from me...I will turn the other cheek, I will forgive and go on forgiving.

I will give and go on giving.

'No matter what any man does to me I will never seek to do harm to him; I will never set out for revenge; I will always seek nothing but his highest good.' [1]

Really?

You kid me!

But this is what the King, born in a stable, came to show us and work in us.

Unconditional love, acceptance and forgiveness.

How can we be any different?

We have His DNA.

We have come under the discipline and desire of the Holy Spirit, whose task it is to *'conform us to the image of Jesus.'* [2]

Transforming our natural, self-referential nature into His self-emptying nature:

The School of the Spirit

'Who thought it not robbery to empty Himself...'[3]

Living our lives as givers not takers, giving Him and everyone else our best...

The first commandment: love Him first, then go on to love everybody else in the way He loves you...

Just like the Master – laying down our lives so that others may benefit...

Hey!

Wait a minute!!

I thought this was about me getting my needs met, living happily ever after and getting all my prayers answered.

Well it is:

"Seek first [and only] *the kingdom of God and His righteousness and all these things will be added to you"*[4] – there it is in black and white.

Can't odds it.

It's a promise...

But it's got a condition attached.

Seek first, **only**, Him and His agenda, His ways... **then**, everything...nothing lacking...everything the world is after, will come to you. But first...seek Him...and His ways...not what you can get...

'And they argued amongst themselves who would be greatest'.[5]

The fallen human condition, me first.

Maybe it's because we never did understand we are a company of people never before seen on the earth – God, is **IN** us.

We are **NOT** ordinary.

We are extraordinary.

We serve another King...

And the law of His domain is not, "What's in it for me?" But "How can I bless you?" And, "What do I have that I can give you?"

Such as I have – I give...

The sign of an open hand and an open heart towards God and man.

Here it is again.

He just doesn't **THINK** like we do!

Notes

1. William Barclay, *New Testament Words* (Louisville, 1974), 21-2.
2. NIV Romans 8:28 – 32
3. Philippians 2:6
4. Matthew 6:33.
5. Luke 22:24 NIV

11 The Two Monks

Have you heard the story of the two monks? They both had a garden and in the garden they both planted a tree.

The one fed and watered his tree, tended it and generally did everything he could to protect it from wind, frost and harsh weather thus enabling it, he thought, to grow and bear fruit.

It died.

The other monk planted his tree and left it.

He let the frost come without protecting it.

The winds too blew against it.

The sun shone on it and baked it and the rains watered it.

It fruited copiously.

Moral?

If we try to protect ourselves from the storms of life we will wither and produce no fruit, it is only the tree that has withstood the elements; put down roots that hold it in the harshest storms; allows the north wind of circumstances; the rain and the sunshine, good days and bad that uses them to grow up and profit, that bears fruit...

We are a company of people emerging in the nation who will live in the way that God does; who will start to demonstrate a love that is not of this world because it belongs to a different place, a different dimension.

It's called the Kingdom of Heaven.

"The kingdom of heaven is like..."[8]

Take a look for yourself what it is like; at Christmas when you celebrate the birth of the King could be a good time to take a peep...

Note
1. Matthew 13

12 Delight

When discipline and desire get married, they produce delight...

Delight follows this union as sure as day follows night.

Light comes with the dawn.

After the butterfly has struggled out of the chrysalis it is delighted with freedom.

That's us.

When we have fought against our old self and won, delight is the result.

Ecstasy.

In the truest sense of the word.

Freedom.

'It is for freedom that Christ has set us free...'[1]

Our old nature held us back; it continually impeded our forward movement until we threw it off.

Like a skin that we need to discard, we cannot soar into the heavenly places and live there while it clings to us.

The anointing always breaks the yoke.

We have become so powerful against ourselves we cannot help but win, when we go out against the enemy.

You can't take ground from the enemy if he has ground in you...

Now we have no enemies but one.

Satan.

And he is defeated.

We fight from a place of victory not towards it. We live in forgiveness.

Living by faith reigning in life...

Now we have security, significance and self-worth the like of which we never could have dreamed.

Our confidence isn't in ourselves but in Him who with His own blood bought us and brought us to Himself.

Weeping may have endured for a night but joy has come in the morning.

We **ARE** overcomers on our way to being more than conquerors...

No good days or bad days any more, only days of grace in which we allow ourselves to be made more and more like Him...embracing the cross, we envisage the crown, but only that we may give it to Him on that day.

Our change of focus is complete – He is our Lodestar – our eyes are on Him alone, our King and coming Bridegroom. We can say with the maiden in the Song of Songs, *"I am His, and I know He desires me..."*[2]

Perfect submission, all is at rest.

All done, got the idea.

Perfected at last...

Amen and Amen and Amen.

Uh, just a moment though, what we have just done was a whistle-stop tour of the Christian life.

Perhaps we might need a bit more explanation, some examples and experience?

Don't forget to tell the Holy Spirit you want to sign up for more...that is if you are sure that you do...you know the cost now...but of course you will carry on reading you're hooked, that's how He does it.

'Therefore I will allure her and speak tenderly to her and give her back her vineyards of fruitfulness.' [3]

Notes
1. Galatians 5:1 NIV
2. Song of Songs 2:16 NIV
3. Hosea 2:14 NIV

13 Review

At the end of a full and fruitful life the man who said, *'It pleased God to reveal his Son in me,'*[1] is crying out: *'that I may know Him,'*[2] which must indicate that with all he had experienced and seen, even being caught up into the third heaven, he knows nothing yet, compared with what there is to be known.

It is humbling to see that we too know so little.

That our constant cry should be the same, "That I may know **You**..."

God answers such a heartfelt prayer.

He loves to make things real in our experience.

Not just theory, which we looked at previously, but authenticity, reality.

He fleshes it out.

He loves to make real in our everyday life, what He has shown us in a place of quiet devotion, so it is that place we need to look at first.

There we need to review how we see Him...

Let's recap first:

We have discovered nothing comes to us in a place of rush or hurry.

We must s *l o w* down.

We are here to learn of Him.

He's different from us...

We need to learn how He likes to order things in the world of His heart.

To live out the law of the Kingdom – the royal law of love in our everyday lives.

To do these things we need to learn how to stay, dwell, and remain, where He has put us.

To...

Be still.

Remain, where He has put us, in Christ.

The School of the Spirit

Become ever more conscious of His indwelling us and our dwelling in Him, and being a partaker of His nature.

We are discovering how to turn and yield our hearts to Him throughout the day, staying connected...

Learning to remain joyful and thankful no matter what our circumstances may look like.

We are discovering we have an internal well of anointing which He fills in our quiet time with Him.

So the first essential to a deeper life in the Spirit is spending quality time with Him.

We all have the same 24 hours, it depends how we divide them... it's called priorities...

Time to review ours.

Put Him first.

So we begin to see all of life through the eyes of His goodness...

In the Secret Place, you and Him alone: in solitude, silence, stillness, simplicity, where surrender and submission are all to be found.

But, here's the 'but' and here's the 'd' word – it's a discipline...

You won't get anywhere without it.

It's conditional.

"As you spend time with Me, I will reveal Myself and My favour towards you..."

Irresistible...

"You are My treasured possession."

Welcome to the Secret Place of His desire and intention towards you...

'I will allure her'.[3]

Are you ready to be allured?

Sure?

Then collect your hard hat here!

Fasten your seatbelt!

Let's go!!!

Nothing will ever be the same again...

He's restoring the Creator/creature relationship...

Notes
1. Galatians 1:16 NIV
2. Philippians 3:10 NIV
3. Hosea 2:14 NIV

14 Circumstances – What If?

We're hitting the road running with this one – our current circumstances. We need to find out how He sees the situation we are in.

The bleaker it is, the more urgent our quest.

Let's do that before we go any further.

We stated that, **'He allows in His wisdom what He could easily prevent by His power.'** [1]

Yes, He could wave a magic wand over your situation and change it immediately but you would encounter and experience nothing of Him if He did.

You would simply be delivered from that circumstance.

"That's what I want", I hear you say. "Get me out of here and make it quick".

Really?

What if – everything around your life right now could be for your profit; your increase; your upgrade; your advantage; your empowering; and by being delivered out of it you would miss a major growth opportunity?

What if?

What if God uses everything in and around your life for a purpose and that purpose is that you might **KNOW** Him, really, really, know Him.

As He really, really is.

Not how you imagine He is...

So you're beginning to see the wisdom that comes from above.

Everything is designed to push you into His arms.

The One who knows you best, loves you best.

And because all this is relational, you can start asking questions of Him, having a dialogue and understanding the process...what it is for...

The School of the Spirit

Questions like:

What does this mean?

What should I do?

Am I reaping what I have sown?

Is this You?

Is this the devil?

Are you nailing something in my life?

Is this the cross?

Am I missing something?

He will tell you.

In this dialogue you will discover the kind intention of His heart, is that you might profit.

Gain, increase, grow, mature, overcome, and conquer... yourself, your circumstances and the enemy.

Cool.

What if…

God is the kindest Person you will ever, ever know?

Question is; have you ever really got to know Him?

What if this dire circumstance… what if this strait place… has a purpose?

And a good purpose at that.

What if this is your starting place?

What if this is your stepping stone into life in the Spirit?

What if!

Just a thought...you might like to think about the possibilities; the 'what if's' that are there in your current situation in the light of it...

Note
1. From the audio study Way of the Warrior by Graham Cooke

15 Knowing His Ways

From now on I think I need to issue a 'health warning'. I would mislead you if I said this was going to be an easy journey.

The deeper life, life in the Spirit, can feel narrow, painful, constricting and difficult – to the old man, the old nature.

But the new man, your spirit man, thrives on it.

The first lessons we learn are:

His ways are not our ways.

He is the Creator, we are the created.

He initiates, we respond.

He allows in His wisdom what He could easily prevent by His power.

We lose to gain; die to live; and the way up, is down.

"Except a corn of wheat fall to the ground and die, it abides alone."[1]

It doesn't reproduce.

It's barren.

Loss is the way to gain.

Death is the way to life.

The way up is down.

Humble yourself that He might exalt you.

"Seekest thou great things for thyself?" Jeremiah said to his scribe Baruch, *"Seek them not"*.[2]

This kingdom is an upside down place.

The sure thing is that if we try to exalt ourselves or hang on to things and people we stunt not only their growth but our own...It depends how dependent you are (if you see what I mean) how easily you will release people, places, things...if they happen to look like being lost.

Life in the Spirit is about displacement.

Two things cannot occupy the same space.

No longer two lives to be lived but one.

For me to live is Christ.

That security blanket; those savings for a rainy day; those bits and bobs of precious china; family heirlooms, jewels...If they occupy your heart, they are likely to come under scrutiny.

They may not, but they might.

You might have to let them go...*'except a man forsake all that he has...he cannot...'*[3]

You can have them back when you can let them go.

When you become a steward not an owner...

And they left **ALL** and followed Him.

"Uh!" I hear you say, "This isn't the picnic I thought it was going to be. What about all this abundant life stuff? That's what I'm after; houses, cars, holidays, healing..."

I think you joined the wrong parade sweetheart!

The truth when it first comes is usually negative!

Notes
1. John 12:24 KJV
2. Jeremiah 45:5 KJV
3. Luke 14:33

16 Experiencing God

As we travel along this highway we find increasingly that we relate everything around us to the work of the Spirit within us.

Our God consciousness goes up.

We discover He can't do through us what He hasn't been able to do in us.

Everything therefore turns to profit for us.

Good, bad, or downright ugly, we can use our day-to-day experiences to learn more of Him...

No good days, no bad days, only days of grace, spent in His abiding presence.

'A man with an experience is beyond reason.' [1]

If you have experienced God; his great heart; His healing power; His deliverance; His kiss; His embrace – you are beyond reason.

No one can talk you out of it.

You know it happened, you experienced it.

Your heart is captivated.

It happened to you.

You are falling in love...

God wants you to not just know about Him and His works, but know **HIM,** His ways.

Up front and personal... How He thinks, how He likes to do things.

He is relational.

You are His inheritance and He is yours.

'All I have – is yours...' [2]

Ever thought about that one??

We are entering the flaming heart of God which burns for you, not against you...though sometimes it may not **feel** like it.

But what do **feelings** have to do with it?

The School of the Spirit

This is where we experience the white-hot passion of God the Creator, for that which He created.

We begin to understand what it means *'to set our faces as flint...'* [3]

And follow Him.

Wherever He goes.

His love, received by us, ignites us with a holy fire; it gives us a blazing heart that burns but is not consumed, with the same things with which His heart is consumed.

'We love because He first loved us' [4]

The direction of our love changes.

What we set our affections on changes us – as Paul explained in Colossians 3:1-17

Paul said, *"I have promised you to one husband, to Christ".* [5]

The Holy Spirit indwells us to make us His own.

Experientially.

He sets us apart.

Yearns jealously over us...

We discover that we are His possession.

In turn, we desire to be possessed.

"The Lord's servant was possessed by God," it was said of Rees Howells by his son, Samuel.

From seeing Him as something we have acquired, possess and seek to use for our advantage – like the maiden early in the Song of Solomon – we come to the place of acceptance and total dependence – *'I am my Beloved's and His desire is towards me...'*[6] we are leaning on the Beloved.

She has completely changed her position – before she had held Him, now, His hold on her is as strong as death...and she knows it.

This then is our journey.

Into the flaming heart and passion of God for us, for me, for you…

Into a life less ordinary.

Because –

'You are His treasure, a holy nation, His people, the people of His power, the people of His passion, the people of His heart, the people of His affection; you are more glorious than you know, stronger than you look, more brilliant than you can imagine – this is your identity; this is who you are – do not permit anybody to talk you out of it or talk you down from that high place, that high calling. You are in Christ, you are astonishing; and at the very least

you are wonderful, His marvellous darling...' [7]

That's Graham Cooke...

On the button as always...

Notes
1. Abbreviated from Leonard Ravenhill: *A man with experience of God is never at the mercy of a man with an argument*
2. Luke 15:31
3. Isaiah 50:7
4. 1 John 4:19 NIV
5. 2 Corinthians 11:2 NIV
6. Song of Solomon 7:10
7. From the audio study *The Art of Thinking Brilliantly* by Graham Cooke

17 Waiting

I suppose one of the earliest and hardest lessons we learn, and one we go on learning is – He is more interested in timing, than time.

So often we feel He's late – again.

Late in our estimation any way.

But we remember His ways aren't ours...

He doesn't measure time, He measures growth...ah!

We want to 'just add hot water and stir'.

Done!

"Get me out of here – like *NOW*!"

We live in an instant society.

He thinks camel, we're thinking Concord!

Let's get this show on the road!

Let's get there!!

He, on the other hand wants to enjoy the journey; take in the scenery; He's not in a hurry, He's enjoying your company...He loves every connection He has with you.

Really?

Yes. Really.

Learning to wait well is a skill we had better try to perfect as soon as possible because so much of our time will be taken up with doing just that – waiting.

Joseph is a good example, he'd spent time in jail and the baker and the wine steward were there with him.

Comes dream time, one is to lose his life; one is to be reinstated...

Joseph can't resist it.

'Remember me when you stand before the Pharaoh...'[1]

You just missed it Joe!

Cost him another two years…

Until he was perfected in the art of, waiting well, his soul was laid in iron...

Without question; without grumbling; without chafing at the bit...

Waiting...

How's it working out for you?

Note
1. Genesis 40:14

18 Knowing Him

"That I may know Him,"[1] Paul says.

That is the essence of a life governed by the Holy Spirit.

It is a life that will deliver us from death; from spiritual stagnation; from going round and round; from coming to a standstill; from being lukewarm.

There is no stopping in the Spirit.

He is restoring the Creator/creature relationship. He's putting it back in the right order.

Man is not top dog.

God is.

One of the major lessons we have to learn in this school and learn well is that He starts things, we respond. He initiates we respond – and sometimes we have it quite the wrong way round...so He has to make a correction.

"All your current circumstances are now compatible with My desire for you".

Ouch!

Before you run away from that thought as your circumstances are negative, maybe even life threatening, and therefore how can that be? Remember you are in the School of the Spirit being prepared like Esther for sharing a throne. The difference is you will be reigning with the King of Kings... nothing as incredible as *that* comes cheaply.

Another lesson we learn here, is that God allows in His wisdom what He could easily prevent by His power...

We are now training in the School of Wisdom, which is the School of the Spirit.

Nothing will turn out the way we expect.

Life could get difficult.

He'll likely offend your mind to get to your heart.

He just doesn't see things the way we do...

His thoughts are not our thoughts.

The School of the Spirit

Nor are His ways our ways.

Right at the front end then, we are challenged about how we see Him.

What our expectation is of Him...

Is He some sort of celestial bellhop or Father Christmas maybe? Or even still a babe in a manger – gentle Jesus meek and mild? And in this situation, this difficulty, this stuck place – do I still believe He has my best interests at heart?

Do I really believe He is all powerful?

All knowing?

Unchangeable?

Do I believe He is good?

Answers prayer?

We have to face this first.

What we **THINK** about God is the most important thing in our lives.

But often it's something we *never* think about, or can't reconcile with our circumstances, so we *won't* think about it.

We don't sit down and examine what we believe.

We've seen that life in the Spirit is about displacement.

So let's displace some old mindsets with some brilliant new ones starting with – He loves you with exactly the same passion and intensity that He loves Jesus.

True/false?

Don't make a mental assent.

Answer the question from where you are right now.

Think about what's being said.

"This is My beloved Son in whom I am well pleased"[2]

He said that, before Jesus had done anything...no miracles, nothing.

So, do you have to 'do' something to make Him accept and love you?

If your experience is one of expectations to be met before you receive approval, it's time for a mindset change, a rethink.

You are accepted plus nothing.

You can do nothing to make Him love you more than He does right now...

Instead of expectation you see another 'e' word – **elevation**... He is always calling you to Himself – "Come up higher."

The School of the Spirit

"Let Me love you more…let Me pour more of Myself into you."

You have embarked on a journey into the heart of God; you're not where you were; you're not where you are going to be; but you're on your way.

Any movement in those mindsets yet?

Stick with the programme, do the homework.

Notes
1. Philippians 3:10
2. Matthew 3:17

19 Moving From Base Camp

There was a story recently of Jesus sitting outside a house on a bench, inside there was a party going on, it was in full swing. Suddenly a man put his head round the door and called, "Hey, Jesus, we need you in here, someone wants healing".

Jesus sighed and said, "They don't want Me, they want what I can give them".

There's partying going on in some places, it's not wrong but there's something beyond the party...

Something beyond your needs being met.

Something beyond the warm fuzzy...

Something beyond the healing...

Him.

So my question today is, do you want Him or what He can give you?

There isn't a right answer here.

But your response may give a clue as to whether you are a follower or a disciple.

"You are those who have stayed with Me through My trials,"[1] Jesus said to the disciples.

Followers, you see, turn back...

No disgrace.

No condemnation.

He doesn't do shame, disgrace, or judgement.

But this is going to be a hard road and you need to understand what you are committing to....

Attitude will determine altitude.

Decisions will determine destiny.

It is not about how you start, but how you finish.

You're going to need staying power.

The School of the Spirit

Endurance.

Fortitude.

Everything for an audience of One.

He must be enough.

When your strength fails.

When hope dies.

And only He remains.

Where else can we go?

Well actually we can go to plenty of places, but it is here, at the end of yourself that you find your beginning in Him…

It is here you find that without Him, nothing.

It's true.

Zilch.

Nada.

Nothing.

Face down.

Out of gas.

Physical strength exhausted.

Then He kicks in.

And you begin to know the exhilaration of life in the Spirit...

After the cross – resurrection.

That I must decrease so that He increases.

That **ALL** my fresh springs are in You.

No one else.

You.

You are enough.

All sufficient.

El Shaddai, the breasted One, the Nurturer...the One who sustains and upholds all things...

When He's all you've got, you find out He is all you need...

That'll be Him.

The pantokrator – Almighty God, the One who is ever present in His creation, Jehovah Sabaoth, the Warrior King, the sustainer, provider, defender and nourisher of His people...

One with Him is always a majority.

The School of the Spirit

How's it working out for you then?

Still up for the climb?

We need to leave base camp...

But He'll be climbing with us so there's nothing to fear.

Note
1. Luke 22:28

20 For Me To Live Is Christ...

'For me to live is Christ...'[1] I'll let you finish the quotation.

Sweet sentiment.

Like the words.

What if He wants to make them real?

Uh?

Yep, exchange – your life for His.

That where we're headed.

That you might do greater works than He did...greater being more, not bigger.

But there's a condition – something has to give.

Two things can't occupy the same space...

He can't do through you what He hasn't been able to do in you.

Coming clear?

It's real.

If He is to do through you what He wants to do, it must happen on the inside of you.

First.

Internal.

Not external.

No paint and wallpaper.

No makeover...

Life in the Spirit is internal.

If you are to be like Him in nature and character – 'something's gotta give' [2] as the old song goes.

All the promises are 'yes' and 'amen' – but only *'in Him'*. [3]

Back where we started...

Him.

The School of the Spirit

Jesus.

Everything comes to the Jesus in us.

Outside of Him – zilch, nada, nothing.

In Him, all things.

'Of Him and to Him and through Him are all things'[4]

It doesn't come to the old man.

It comes to the new, the Jesus in you.

So how real is your experience of the new man within?

Do you understand the war that broke out the moment you believed?

There is another King...

We spoke about Him before.

Now He's making it real.

He has so much He wants you to have.

He's going to establish you in exactly who you are.

A son.

Then when He's satisfied you've really, really, got it.

He's going to move you on to servant-hood, friendship and finally you'll become His love slave...

But first...

First, He wants to make sonship real – in your experience.

It's all about taking Him at His word.

Believing what He says.

And uh – obedience.

Delayed obedience is disobedience they say...

So where are you today, beloved of God?

Notes
1. Philippians 1:21
2. From the song: Johnny Mercer, Something's Gotta Give
3. 2 Corinthians 1:20
4. Romans 11:36

21 The Holy Spirit

"When the He [Holy Spirit] *comes… He will glorify and honour Me…and disclose it to you," Jesus said.*[1]

When you enter His school it's all about Jesus.

He will always bring you back to Him.

That's the role of the Holy Spirit in your life, to reveal Christ to you and in you.

It's His job.

'When He [the Holy Spirit] *comes…He will guide you into all the truth…For He will speak whatever He hears* [from the Father…regarding the Son] *and disclose it to you…'*[2]

That doesn't resonate too well with us, because it is right here we find out how self-referential we are.

Everything relates to how it affects little 'ole me...

If you don't believe me, who do you look for first in a group photo?

Answers on a postcard please.

The Holy Spirit's job is to kill you off!

He has the same agenda as the devil; they both want to kill you, but for different reasons.

One of them is measuring you for a coffin, the other for a blessing...

The devil comes to *'kill, steal and destroy'*.[3]

The Holy Spirit has come that you might experience the abundance Jesus spoke about in John 10:10; that His life might become your life, in fullness, not measure.

Please understand that God knows the pain that you've gone through.

He knows the difficulties.

He knows what it's cost you.

Every trial of your faith.

The thing that grieves Him is you've gone through all this grief and this pain and you haven't understood what

He wanted to give you.

Or what He wanted to be for you.

You haven't found Him in them.

Israel went through all manner of stuff and each time they were hard up against it, God stepped in and showed them another aspect of Himself that they could experience.

Jehovah Nissi – a fight on their hands and He's there, as a banner, assuring them of victory. Jehovah Rohi, the Lord who shepherds me; Jehovah Sabaoth, the Warrior King who fights for them...

You went through all that and you didn't hold on to God because all you did was look at the circumstances.

The Holy Spirit is here to make sense, perfect sense, of everything you have experienced and make it work *for* you beloved.

'*To give you a hope and a future*'.[4]

Guaranteed.

He's said so.

To give you a major victory in the place of your greatest defeat.

He is the resident genius of heaven sent to you to enable you to do anything and everything God asks of you.

What a gift.

'But the Helper, the Holy Spirit, whom the Father will send in My name, He will teach you all things…'[5]

Thank you Jesus.

Notes
1. John 16:13 AMP
2. John 16:13 AMP
3. John 10:10
4. Jeremiah 29:11
5. John 14:26

22 Going Around It One More Time...

God repeats Himself.

It is said that if an editor looked at the Bible he could cut it by a third, the reason being that God repeats Himself.

He says the same thing time and time again...

I wonder why?

Anyone who has been a parent will know that a child doesn't learn about danger at the first warning.

We have to repeat that warning again, and again, and again, and again, until they get it.

Really get it and stop whatever it is they shouldn't be doing.

We are insisting, "Doing that will hurt you, stop it."

God is exactly the same.

Just look at His warnings to Israel in the Old Testament..."If you do this, I am going to have to do that...because what you are doing will hurt you".

He sent His prophets, time and again.

Warning.

They didn't listen.

"Who do you think you are, telling me what to do?"

"I don't think I'm anyone but God is saying..."

"Go away!"

"Shut up!"

God told Jeremiah, "They won't listen to a word you say".

("Don't help me Lord!")

"But you keep telling them anyway..."

They didn't listen, just like He said.

They ended up in the fifth cycle of discipline, dispossessed, scattered from their homeland and in captivity...

Question is, are we any better?

The School of the Spirit

Do we pay any more attention?

The epistles you know are just repeats in a different way of what Jesus had already said...

"Love Me first, then love one another as I have loved you," for example. Simply the first commandment…

Do we?

I think not, not in the true agape sense of the word anyway, the best we can manage is, "You scratch my back I'll scratch yours..." and that includes Him!!! "You answer my prayers Lord and I'll serve you, if it suits me".

We do have a habit of 'compassing the mountain' a number of times before we go 'straight'.

Seriously, what circumstance are you currently going around that you have been around many times before?

You could walk it with your eyes closed; it's just the people or place, which is different.

Same situation, same way marks, only the names 'have been changed to protect the innocent' as they used to say...

Wake up Oh child of God, He is showing you it is time to hear what He is saying in this situation where yet again you have the same attitude or mindset towards the people or places... or even Him; time to stop compassing this mountain and go straight?

Can't afford to waste any more precious time my beloved, justifying why you are stuck there...

In the nicest possible way I can say it; lovingly as I can – just cut us all some slack and move your feet eh sweetheart?

Prophets again...

"Telling us what to do..."

"Who do they think they are?"

Nothing changes...

"But you, Jeremiah, keep telling them..."

23 God Is Cyclical

What I mean by that is – He thinks in circles.

Not straight lines.

He isn't linear as we are.

We read a book; start at the beginning and go through to the end.

We catch a train and get to our destination.

Straight lines.

He thinks, "All things start with Me and end with Me."

Circle.

'I am the Alpha and the Omega….

The beginning and the end...'[1]

And everything in between I may add...

So He thinks circular; He thinks journey; He thinks *"of Him and to Him and through Him are all things".*[2]

It's a circle and it passes through you at some point.

Because you are in Christ, you are part of the circle.

When He calls you to Himself, He puts sonship at the top of the circle – His priority is relationship.

So the first thing He will establish in you is the fact that you are His child.

You belong to His family.

By blood.

You have a new DNA.

He no longer addresses you outside of that.

Everything comes to you in your position as a new-born child of God.

A new-born with the potential to become a fully mature son.

He doesn't put you to work...I want you to retain that thought. Why, will become clear; suffice to say, with Him the rule is always...

The School of the Spirit

Relationship before function.

That in a nutshell is now your life journey.

Going from a child to a fully mature son, **always** in relationship.

Everything with Him is relational.

Nothing outside of that.

You are in Him.

And He is in you.

That is about as relational as you can get.

But growth doesn't happen overnight; it doesn't in the natural and it doesn't in the spiritual.

It doesn't happen outside of being in Him.

Staying where HE has put you.

In His Son.

HE is in you and you are in Him.

Double wrapped.

All things come to the Jesus in you.

Takes years.

Slow down.

In Israel a man wasn't considered to be fully mature until he was thirty...*'Jesus, being about thirty years old...went forth.'*[3]

Some of us are more than thirty years old in the Lord, but we have never had anyone explain before, there is a growth process to be gone through, and it takes time, because we have a destiny and a purpose.

If that's you, prepare for a revelation of just who you are.

Royalty.

You are currently in training for reigning.

God is very intentional towards you.

He has a purpose and a destiny for you.

He never speaks to you outside of what He sees you can **become**.

You are always becoming something beloved...

He is always present future with you, not present past.

If you know all this already, go and have a coffee or something...while I chat to those of you to whom this is all new...you can pick up with us later.

We start around this circle then, with Him establishing us

securely in His love, acceptance and affection for us.

We now have three things that cannot be taken away from us:

SECURITY

SIGNIFICANCE and

SELF-WORTH

Security, significance and self-worth.

We have a destiny and a purpose.

All the things the world seeks are given to us freely.

We can stop fretting.

Start believing and receiving what everybody else strives for.

It's just been given to us.

Done.

Dusted.

We are citizens of another kingdom; the world is now our oyster.

We will return to the top of this circle, sonship, many times during our journey as we grow up and on into adulthood.

But first, ***first***, He wants you to know how safe you are.

He's got you.

You have changed both direction and parents.

You are part of His Royal Family.

You are now in training for reigning.

We'll look at the next stopping place in the cycle but you can be certain of one thing, He will keep you in this place until He is completely satisfied that you know ***who*** you are and ***Whose*** you are...however long that takes.

Isn't He lovely?

And aren't you precious?

And isn't this life is really worth living (and dying) for?

We've only just begun.

It gets much better.

If you received only half a Gospel, read on!

Notes
1. Revelation 22:13
2. Romans 11:36
3. Luke 3:23

24 Servanthood

So we lingered on sonship in the previous section and I said He wouldn't move you around to the next place in the circle until He was absolutely sure you had really 'got' it: got who you are and to Whom you belong.

You really, *really* have changed parents.

You really, *really* have a new life.

You really, *really* are a new creation.

You are now a citizen of a different nation, a different kingdom, the Kingdom of Heaven.

Everything will come to you in this place.

You fight from the victory Jesus won on the Cross, not towards it.

No one can shift you from this position.

You have three things remember?

Can you tell me what they are?

Ok, jog the memory.

You have: security, significance and self-worth.

You are not where you were, you are not where you are going to be, but you are on your way.

You have seen that God is circular in His thinking, everything comes from Him and goes back to Him and you are there in the middle...that He always sees what you can become, not what you currently are.

So when He has fully established you in your place as a much-loved child, not before, He moves you into servanthood.

Everything flows from relationship – without that firmly in place, He will not move you into service.

Your fellows may, your leaders may, but He will not.

In this part of the circle, you learn to serve properly under His careful tuition; under the watchful eye of the Holy Spirit, not with a hidden agenda.

Not with an ulterior motive – like how can I move in my gifting here?

But serve.

Clean the toilets.

Make the tea.

Love the people...

Uh?

Yes, love them, the good, the bad and the downright ugly – warts and all!

Because He does.

Here you learn to suffer interruption of your plans.

Discomfort.

Maybe even deprivation.

Think about Joe again for a moment here, he is a really good example.

Gets this prophecy while he's wet behind the ears, mouths it off to anyone within range, and the next thing he's down a hole – very funny guys, ok game's up.

But it wasn't.

It was the start of his training to become what God saw.

A man to whom He could entrust the welfare of a vast nation, Egypt.

Second only to Pharaoh.

Joe suffered all right.

We are told his soul was laid in iron.

But he developed the right mindset and attitudes; he held no one accountable for his predicament, he saw that it was all working for good...

So in this place of servanthood you will learn as he did, that *'all things work together for good for those who love God, who are the called according to His purpose'.*[1]

Key words, *'called according to HIS purpose'.*

Not yours.

It's in this place that all self-seeking and self-serving dies; that you only want Him and what He wants.

Here you learn what it means to be aligned with Him and really serve Him – wherever He chooses to place you, and do it willingly with a smile on your face...no matter what.

Takes time...for some, longer than others.

But He makes sure we don't move on to the next staging post until we are ready.

The School of the Spirit

Life in the Spirit isn't for the faint-hearted, beloved.

It will cost you everything you have, He did warn you.

But it will bring you into a place in the Spirit you could not even dream about...

Come on; let's keep going with this thing.

We can't lose can we?

Note
1. Romans 8:28.

25 Friendship

"Henceforth… I have called you friends,"[1] Jesus said to His disciples.

He didn't say it to the multitudes, but to those who had been with Him and stayed with Him during His trials, there weren't many of them – 12 and one of them would betray Him.

So the next staging post is friendship.

Friendship sounds lovely; when He called me there for the first time I was terrified.

I kept seeing it and backing away.

I think it was the degree of intimacy it implied.

You share your deepest thoughts and emotions with those you call friends; those whom you know you can trust...

So friendship for me, with Him, was a trust issue.

Not me trusting Him.

Him trusting me.

That's what scared me.

He is sharing His heart with me because He trusts me.

That is what frightened me.

"God is giving you this because He trusts you..."

"God is giving you these people to look after because He trusts you with them."

Prophetic words kept coming, scaring me witless.

God, do you know what you are doing???

He pushes you into a place of ever deepening dependence and intimacy.

Where you find, by experience, that without Him you can do nothing.

Zilch.

Nada.

Nothing.

The School of the Spirit

Do you remember how I said He always likes to make things real in our experience?

He teaches you something – information.

Then by experience – revelation.

Or the other way around.

But it's always, relational.

It's always about you and Him.

You learning His ways; how He likes to order things in the world of His heart; how He sees people and situations; how He sees you...

How He sees His will being accomplished on earth as it is in heaven – through you.

Essentially that is the sole responsibility we have in this thing, to do the will of Him who chose us and sends us...

Purpose.

Destiny.

In the end...

Rewards for a job well done.

Whether you are a butcher, a baker, a candlestick maker, a

mum, a dad, a teacher, a judge...whatever your calling...just do it to the best of your ability and He will do the rest.

It's a fallacy you know that there is a difference between the sacred and the secular.

He makes no such distinction.

He drops us down in circumstances and says, "Nevertheless, I will be with you."

And one with Him is a majority.

What confidence that engenders.

He is with us.

He is for us.

He calls us into friendship because He wants to tell us His plans...He always tells His servants the prophets beforehand what He plans to do.

Check it out.

Next step then – slavery.

We'll look at that next, if you feel strong enough that is…

Note
1. John 15:15 KJV

26 Slavery

This one always elicits a gulp!

It shouldn't do.

Paul frequently referred to himself as a slave of Christ, a slave of the gospel, or a love slave.

It's just that we have a tendency to gloss over what he's saying to get to the next bit.

It originates from the Jewish tradition of a slave who was due to be freed, going to the master whom he loved and asking him if he could stay there with him...

The master would then take the servant, pierce his ear by driving an awl through the earlobe to the doorpost of the dwelling, then placing a ring in the hole that showed everybody what the slave had chosen. It was a witness to the goodness of the master as well as the loyalty of the slave.

Never to leave his master.

To serve him until he died.

'Pierce my ear O Lord my God, take me to Your throne this day, I will serve no other God...Lord, I'm here to stay.' [1] Was an old chorus that we used to sing, little understanding where it originated or what it meant.

So, after sonship, servanthood, and friendship, comes the invitation to be His love slave.

Before you think you could *lose* anything by taking this position let me assure you it is the place

where you *gain* most.

It is where you have learned in the School of the Spirit that perfect love, His love perfected in you,

casts out fear.

Where you are beginning to see what agape looks like.

You are living in it and passing it on.

Your world is at His feet.

Always with Him.

The School of the Spirit

Never alone.

Not your capability, His ability.

Perfect submission.

Absolute confidence in Him.

All is at rest.

The maiden in the Song of Songs learned this – she ends up coming from the wilderness, leaning on the beloved...

That's the place.

Putting all your weight on Him.

He will never force you into this position – it's voluntary.

You have decided to follow Him.

To be a disciple.

Not a believer or a follower, they turned back.

You move, ever deeper, deeper into the love of Jesus.

One with Him.

Union.

No longer two wills but one.

His.

His ways surely aren't our ways, but they are lovely.

Note
1. From the song: Steve Croft Pierce My Ear

27 His Ways

Whoa!

We need to slow down a little and take a diversion for a moment to look at His ways, which are so lovely, and what we can do practically to align ourselves with them, as we become disciples.

We will look in a moment about how God thinks in terms of timing, not time, but as we are locked in time, we need to examine that first, at least, how we use it.

Time, that is.

To do this, we will need to develop some spiritual disciplines like: stillness; silence; solitude; simplicity; submission and eventually, surrender...

Lovely words, but first problem, I don't have time –

'I went out Lord, men were coming out, they were coming and going, Lord, walking and running, everything was rushing, cars, lorries, the street, the whole town. Men were rushing not to waste time; they were rushing after time, to catch up with time, to gain time.

Goodbye sir, Excuse me, I'll come back, I can't wait, haven't time.

Must end this letter – but I haven't time.

I'd love to help you but I haven't time,

Can't accept, having no time.

I can't think, can't read, I'm swamped, haven't time.

I'd like to pray but I haven't time.

You understand Lord, they simply haven't the time.

The child is playing; he hasn't the time right now, later on...

The school boy has his homework to do; he hasn't the time, later on...

The student has his courses and so much work; he hasn't time, later on...

The young married man has his new house, he has to fix it up, he hasn't time, later on...

The grandparents have their grandchildren; they haven't time, later on...

They are ill, they have their treatments, they haven't time, later on...

They are dying...they have no...

Too late, they have no more time...

And so all men run after time Lord, they pass through life running, hurried, jostled overburdened, frantic – and they never get there, in spite of all their efforts, they still are – short of time.

Lord, you must have made a mistake in your calculations, there's a big mistake somewhere, the hours are too short, our lives are too short. You who are beyond time Lord, you smile to see us fighting it, You know what You are doing. You make no mistakes in Your distribution of time to man, you give each one time to do what You want him to do, but we mustn't lose time, waste time, kill time, pass time, for time is a gift that you give us, but a perishable gift that doesn't keep Lord.

Lord, I have time, I have plenty of time, all the time you give me, the years of my life, the days of my years, the hours of my days, they are all mine, mine to fill, quietly, calmly, but to fill completely up to the brim, to offer them to You that out of their insipid water You may make a rich wine, such as You once made in Cana of Galilee.

I'm not asking You today Lord for time to do this and then that, but Your grace to do conscientiously, in the time that You give me, what You want me to do.' [9]

Michel Quoist

Note
1. Michel Quoist, *Prayers* (London 1954) p96 Used with kind permission of Gill Publishing Dublin

28 Time

Here we go then.

Time.

The commodity we all have, but few manage well.

I guarantee there were some wry smiles as you read Michel Quoist yesterday on the subject.

But we have to address this whole issue of time.

And what we do with it.

Because if we are to be significant in these *end times*, we will have to develop the ability to use our time much more wisely than we do at present…

As Michel Quoist says so succinctly, currently we waste it; use it; pass it; and heaven forbid, kill it…

What an indictment.

Twenty-four hours in every day and we still waste most of it.

May I suggest before we start you stop right there and consider what use you currently make of the only commodity you *really* have, and that you can never get back – time.

Then we can look at some particulars…

29 Time – to Be Still

Take time right now – To be *still*…

Ah, stillness, now there's a thought…some of us find it quite impossible to be still. If I were a betting person I would guess you are finding it difficult right now to be still long enough to read these few lines…

It actually takes time to get us still.

When we first try it, we fail miserably and usually give up after about ten minutes – if that.

Perseverance is something we will have to develop too.

Stillness isn't found in a hurry – no pun intended.

'Take time to be holy,

Speak oft with thy Lord' [1]

That's an old hymn…

Time, again.

It goes on to say, **'the world rushes on'** [2] doesn't it just; but what is it achieving for all its rush and hurry?

Stress, heart attacks, ulcers, grey hair…all those unpleasant things…

We weren't built for stress.

It wasn't in the Designer's mind.

He created man on the sixth day to *rest*.

That's why we labour to enter into it.

It takes…

…time.

Time to be

Still.

Set apart.

Just you and Him.

The School of the Spirit

How He loves this.

Time you set apart just to be with Him.

Asking nothing.

Seeking only that you may sit at His feet in silent contemplation of Him...

Just how long is it since you did that?

Made an appointment to be with Him and kept it for more than five minutes?

You have to make a start somewhere – is now a good time for you?

I sense it is, see you tomorrow.

Don't get up; I'll see myself out...

Notes
1. From the hymn *Take Time to be Holy* by William Dunn Longstaff The United Methodist Hymnal
2. From the hymn *Take Time to be Holy* by William Dunn Longstaff The United Methodist Hymnal

30 Time – In Silence

Wow! Now there's something we find really hard.

Our Martha must be doing something all the time, busy, busy, busy; she can't be still, but *silence*, that's something else again.

Even if she is in the Presence, she's talking, agitating – what shall I read? Shall I put a CD on? How shall I pray? What do I do next?

Even if she appears to be sitting still.

It's all going on inside.

Questions, questions…no stillness…no silence…

Martha, unlike Mary, knows little of these virtues, silence and stillness.

Poor dear, cumbered about with many cares she is.

Martha of course is your soul.

It always has to be producing something or it isn't satisfied, happy or peaceful.

Doing, doing, doing.

As the song goes, '**Be, do, be, do, be, do...**' [1]

You're saying it right now and you are hearing what you are saying – your 'be' must come before your **'do'.**

That isn't going to get out of your mind all day now!

Does it?

I mean, does your 'being' with Him, precede your 'doing' for Him?

If it doesn't, could now be the time for a change?

You can then add silence to the discipline of stillness you have just learnt about.

Just a thought.

Note
1. From the song *Strangers in the Night* as sung by Frank Sinatra, lyrics by Charles Singleton and Eddie Snyder 1966.

31 Time – In Solitude

Poustinia.

Poustinia is a Russian word.

It means desert.

'Poustinia' so called, are little cabins which are built in an area of seclusion.

They are there so you might encounter God in silence, solitude and prayer.

Making poustinia entails going apart from your community to a cabin where you fast and pray in solitude, generally for a day.

Some of us can't abide being on our own for more than five minutes.

We put the TV on, or the radio.

Just to make us feel there's someone there…

There is someone there; it's just that our level of God consciousness is too low to detect His presence…

Solitude is something that forces us to stop and most importantly, listen.

The silence can be deafening.

Put these three together, stillness, silence and solitude, and we have something quite foreign to our 21st century way of living, poustinia.

Desert.

These are the disciplines that He so loves to encourage in us.

Jesus was always taking Himself out into the desert to be alone with the Father.

Because being with Him like that, in reverent silence, produces simplicity…

Life just irons itself out somehow…

That which mattered so much, disappears, as He becomes the subject of our attention and focus.

The School of the Spirit

As we *'set our affections on things above and not on the earth.'* Colossians 3:2

Could I ask you to do that right now please?

Set your affections on Him.

Let your heart go to another place.

Put Him between you and your problem.

You just made poustinia.

Right there where you were, you can practice it any time.

Try it.

It works.

32 Time – To Simplify

What about that.

Simplify.

Our lives are so complicated…

We are told that everything is labour saving, yet we appear to have less time than ever and rush through the day with hardly a breath; some even don't have time to take a lunch break…

What is happening to us?

In a word – we are distracted.

The enemy, if he can't stop us, will distract us.

Cumber us about with all kinds of things we *must* do right this minute.

If you took an honest look at your life right now I'm sure you would discover that 50% of what you say **must** be done right now could be left until later; that might leave some quality time for being with the One Person who really, really matters.

Because what you think about Him is the single most important thing in your life.

Disagree if you will, but you are going to spend eternity with Him, He's your Bridegroom, and now is the time when you can get to know Him…that is, if you can spare the time…

The Westminster Catechism tells us that the chief end of man is to glorify God and enjoy Him forever.

When are you going to start?

Enjoying Him that is?

Is it something you have been putting off every day?

'Fess up.

You know it is.

Everything else takes first place and by the time you have time for Him it is the tail end of the day and you are falling asleep over your Bible reading…

I didn't need a crystal ball for that!

How about it beloved, making some quality time for Him

beloved, He loves every connection He has with you – don't deny Him His pleasure any longer...

He is your inheritance, but you are His also...

He wants His enjoyment too.

33 Time – To Submit

Look at us!

That's another word that has us bristling.

Submission.

Or at least some of the ladies when it is connected to men; more particularly husbands…

But that's another issue.

Submission, we have to learn this gentle art, or we won't get very far in the School.

We took a brief look at the word poustinia or 'desert.'

A place like the Sahara, a lonely place our souls sometimes have to enter, to find the God who dwells within.

Our whole journey is that of learning to bow the knee on the *inside*.

Acknowledging that we are not our own; we were bought at a price; that we are the created and He is the Creator; and we are learning to take our proper place before Him.

In *submission* to Him.

He never forces or coerces us.

He lets us find out that we don't know; we don't understand; we can't comprehend Him and His ways.

Because the more we try the worse it gets:

'Thus says the Lord, "Let not a wise man boast of his wisdom, and let not the mighty man boast of his might, let not a rich man boast of his riches; but let him who boasts boast of this, that he understands and knows Me, that I am the Lord who exercises loving kindness, justice and righteousness on earth; for I delight in these things," declares the Lord.' [1]

Have done with boasting then…

The only secure place is *submission* to the Divine will –

'And Mary said, Behold the handmaid of the Lord; be it unto me according to thy word.' [2]

There is something sublime in these words of the Virgin Mary, as she responds to the news that she is to bear a child conceived by the Holy Ghost…her attitude is one of **perfect** submission.

She has no idea what this is going to mean; except that in the natural, if she is discovered to be pregnant before marriage, she could be stoned to death.

And she's yet to face Joseph with the news…

But she doesn't demur.

"Whatever you say," is her respectful response.

Any wonder she is revered in some circles.

Here is a young girl, probably about 14 years old — demonstrating for all time what submission to the Divine will actually looks like.

A lesson there I think.

It doesn't come naturally to 21st century believers, but we can practice submitting to Him right through our day, if we are really serious about developing this virtue.

When we come up against a situation where we want to retaliate or get angry, just suppose we try submitting to Him, before we let fly…

We might find that the fruit of the Spirit is sprouting forth where once there was anger, bitterness and wrath, now there is peace, joy and love.

Worth a try.

Give it a go for a month and see how you get on.

You won't be disappointed.

Growth guaranteed.

Notes
1. Jeremiah 9:23-24 NASB
2. Luke 1:38 KJV

34 Timing Not Time

One of the unfortunate results of our instant society, as I pointed out earlier in this series, is that we want everything now and we linger and think deeply about very little.

Life in the church community reveals this; we are a mile wide and half an inch deep.

Always after what's new...

There is no substance to us because we have lost the art of meditating, considering, thinking through what we already have.

Remaining with a thought for more than a few seconds...

We have the attention span of a gnat.

God is not like this.

He is agricultural.

He thinks timing, not time.

He sows the seed...

Then He waits...

'First the blade, then the ear, after that the full corn in the ear.'[1]

He has endless patience with us...

Unlike us, when we're dealing with others!

He allows the north and the south winds.

Spring, summer, autumn and winter.

Seasons.

What season are you in in God?

Winter?

Die back after harvest?

Spring?

New growth, possibilities abound...

Summer – harvest, luxuriant growth, goes on forever...

The School of the Spirit

Autumn.

Leaves turning golden and falling off.

Being pruned for greater harvest next year?

Possibilities looking bleak, walls closing in, winter near?

When a tree goes into winter mode it takes all its life back down into its roots.

It's not a time of no growth, but consolidation.

Spring will come again.

The sap will rise.

But it must replenish itself by feeding through its root system.

If it were to try to stay green for twelve months without resting, it would exhaust itself and die...

So how about it beloved?

Do you need to step off the merry-go-round that your life has become?

Take a breather.

Put an X and dig there for a while instead of dashing from one thing to another?

Think deeply maybe about these messages?

Slow down.

Let those who want to run, run.

Tortoise and hare...

The man who stops to sharpen his scythe and the rider who stops to shoe his horse, are not wasting time.

Can't harvest with a blunt scythe.

Can't outrun the enemy with a lame horse...

Point made I think.

God is agricultural.

Seasonal.

Check your season and make sure your lifestyle matches it.

Life in the Spirit is about timing – not time.

Note
1. Mark 4:28 KJV

35 'D' Words

We had an old family saying: "I'll go through fire and water for you but if it's raining, don't expect me!"

We always laughed.

Old jokes are always the best.

How does that relate to today's message?

Which may not even raise a smile...

Time for some 'D' words:

Displacement and

Decisions that

Define us.

God is always about displacement (and replacement).

Displacing our thoughts with His (which you recall are higher than ours) and replacement; replacing a negative mindset with a positive one.

Our history in Him, is one of unlearning what we thought we knew...

It's a bit daunting at first – another 'd' word which doesn't appeal to the ego much – in fact the purpose is to kill the thing, as we've seen before – God and the devil both want to kill you.

For completely different reasons of course.

In the School of the Spirit you die to live.

Requirement number one.

'Except a grain of wheat fall to the ground and die, it abides alone'.[1]

Expect to die.

Die to your plan for your life:

'All my hopes, ambitions, wishes round my feet in ashes lay, then God's fire upon the altar of my heart was set aflame...'[2]

One of the old songwriters of last century...

The School of the Spirit

They talked a lot about...

Consecration and holiness.

Rarely heard these days.

Daniel *'purposed in his heart'.*[3]

Jesus *'set his face like flint'.*[4]

Paul *'determined not to know anything among you, save Jesus Christ, and him crucified,'*...[5]

These are only a few of the many men and women of the Bible who have left us a record of spiritual greatness born out of a will, firmly set to do the will of God....

God doesn't change the way He does things.

He extracts from us in a time of war what we gave Him in a time of peace...

Death doesn't only apply to Jesus but to those who will follow Him.

Into resurrection life.

Otherwise – it's the flesh that we are living from, not the Spirit.

It is possible...

To live in the Spirit...

To live the other side of the cross.

In resurrection life.

But it requires another 'D' word – ***decision*** –

Something happens when you decide to die to yourself.

'For me to live, is Christ, to die is gain'.[6]

He takes over...

No longer two lives to be lived but one – His, through you.

He can't do through you what He hasn't been able to do in you...

One way ticket this.

You begin to live above your circumstances a life less ordinary, where heaven comes down and you get all your prayers answered...

Bonus!

And you walk with Him and talk with Him and are a co-worker with Him...you reign with Him and rule with Him not only in this life, but the one to come.

The dominion given to Adam, and then lost by him, is regained when we live, in where we have been placed, in Christ.

The School of the Spirit

Everything done for an audience of One.

Fancy some of that?

Of course you do!

Stick with the programme!

We've got enough information now to start making some quality decisions – our last 'd' word.

Life choices.

Life changers.

Game changers.

Decisions that define us.

Here we go then:

You need to give Him a blank cheque; sign here:

I promise to give the Lord Jesus Christ anything He asks, do anything He says, and go anywhere He sends. Take my life Lord.

Signed...Date...........

Always useful to commit these things to writing I find...

Are you still there?

Thought I had lost you there for a moment...

Of course I haven't.

Good, that's done let's go on.

Notes
1. John 12:24
2. From the hymn *When I saw the Cleansing Fountain* by Mrs J Harris Redemption Hymnal
3. Daniel 1:8
4. Luke 9:51
5. 1 Corinthians 2:2
6. Philippians 1:21

36 The Government of God

If you are still struggling with the last lesson in the School, and I suspect some of you will be this may help...

All that we have seen is summed up in that one phrase.

The government of God in our lives.

Many of us have never realised what took place when we were born again and baptised.

This lack of understanding has meant we do not co-operate with the Holy Spirit as we should.

When we hear *'for me to live, is Christ, to die is gain'*[1] we think that was just for Paul or some super spiritual people.

But the fact is, the identification you went through when you were fully immersed, was with the death of Christ and therefore His resurrection, that's why Paul told us to reckon ourselves dead to sin but alive to God, in Christ.

When you came up from the water you had undergone a rite of passage that brought you under the Lordship of Christ, under His government, His headship; just as He, following His baptism only ever did what the Father was doing and only ever saw things the way the Father did, so it must be for us.

Your ultimate decision is to agree with something that is already a fact.

When you were baptised you died and your life was hid with Christ in God.[2]

But He never coerces or forces us.

Many souls are saved but never converted.

To be converted means you make an about turn, a complete change in direction.

Many are believers, or followers but not disciples.

Disciples know and understand the full import of the Gospel, the good news, not the mediocre news and they have appropriated all that Christ won for them.

A completely new start.

Not a makeover.

The School of the Spirit

That is what signing that blank cheque means – a new start.

His life for yours.

Everything under His government and control, joy, joy, joy all the way – even though it is difficult at times, you have your constant companion, the Holy Spirit, to teach and guide you.

He's just like Jesus.

It's like walking with Jesus every day.

'I will send you another Comforter.'[3] – Someone who is just like Me.

And He did.

We have all we need to live this thing.

It is true, it takes a lifetime to produce the Christ life in us, but the journey of a thousand miles starts with the first step.

We **do** have a fallen nature that wants to fight back every step of the way.

We **are** rebels at heart.

But He's given us a new one of those...

So we can say, "Yes," to Him and mean it.

He has something very precious He wants us to have.

Dominion.

God wants us to take back that dominion we lost at the Fall.

And He starts with our own inner territory.

Getting control and dominion over ourselves.

So unless we recognise this enmity, this warfare, that rages within and how important it is that we align ourselves with Him in everything, we are doomed to stay in a place where the enemy can use us to play football any time he wishes.

Lunch is served and you are on the menu.

Every time you protect yourself you go into the enemy's territory.

Self-protection.

"I did it my way," [4] was Adam's theme tune.

You can throw a tantrum a week and walk away from God any time if you want to, He won't love you any the less; just be aware that the lovely red carpet and white sofas means you have walked into the lion's mouth...that's his tongue and his teeth you're looking at and the trap is about to close on you – again...

The choice is yours.

You can be **'tossed about with many a conflict many a doubt, fightings within and fears without...'** [5] as the old hymn goes.

The School of the Spirit

Or you can grow up and live in resurrection life, running towards Him every time you have a problem.

Everything we have looked at so far presupposes that you understand this and have made the choice.

That's why I brought you to that place of signing a blank cheque.

So that you might see your own resistance to the government of God.

And make a choice.

God sees you as already dead and risen in Christ, question is, how do you see you?

Getting this sorted could revolutionise your Christian walk and bring great joy as we move on to look at how being in the School of the Spirit will affect every aspect of your life, if you let it. If you want this and embrace it the result will be out of this world...just sign that cheque and we can get started.

Notes
1. Philippians 1:2
2. Colossians 3:1
3. John 14:16 KJV
4. From the song My Way sung by Frank Sinatra in 1969, Songwriters Claude Francois & Jacques Revaux, English lyrics by Paul Anka.
5. From the Hymn: Charlotte Elliott *Just as I Am*

37 Church: An Expression Of The Kingdom

Something else we need to untangle before we go any further is the issue of church versus kingdom.

Unfortunately we have made Church an entity in itself when it is but an expression of the kingdom.

Church grows out of kingdom not the other way around.

Jesus came preaching the Kingdom.

We tend to put a church on every corner that replicates itself.

If someone else is doing something that looks as though it works – we do it – with varying degrees of success...

God doesn't make carbon copies.

He's creative, purposeful, and intentional.

He is purposefully vague about what we do when we meet together because He wants us to stay fresh and alive to Him all the time…

He doesn't do rote, or format...

And Church, as an expression of the kingdom, is meant to meet the need of our particular community.

It's no good starting a playgroup if you have a community in which the majority is old age pensioners.

You're getting my drift.

Life in the Spirit is about finding out what God wants to do and then asking Him to do it.

That applies to us as individuals and groups.

He doesn't use carbon paper – or a photocopier.

It will be different for every person, group and situation.

He sees each one of us as individuals not a blob.

So He has a plan for each of us – all together now, Jeremiah 29:11 – you should know it by heart now.

Life in the Spirit is never boring and it has a much broader scope than church...it's about the kingdom.

The Government.

The School of the Spirit

Of God.

In and through His people.

God is constantly creating new things.

Doing new things.

He knew He couldn't rework the old you so He made a new one.

We've covered that.

Brilliant.

Then He filled that new you with Himself.

The Holy Spirit: heaven's genius, given to us, to live in us while we're on earth.

Without Him you can do nothing of eternal value.

Left to yourself all you would do, would be to reproduce after your own kind...

Another lesson then.

God doesn't make carbon copies – except of course when it comes to the nature of His Son being formed in us.

That's a given.

'That I might be like Him...'[1]

Otherwise, back to Father's drawing board to see what He wants to do with that local expression of kingdom you call church.

You may want to ask Him what it should look like...and suggest some innovative changes perhaps...

Note

1. John 3:2

38 Cycles And Circles

We looked at the fact that God worked in circles and cycles.

We examined the circle of sonship, through servanthood, friendship and finally slavery.

He loves being circular with us.

Because everything starts and ends with Him.

He is more interested in the worker than the work.

Relationship before function.

In each cycle or circle you will experience exactly the same things:

Worship and surrender – as we yield to Him

Pleasure and pain – as the training starts.

Achievement and suffering – as we see His purposes and align ourselves.

Weakness and power – as we decrease and He increases.

We looked at the very first cycle God always establishes, the relational cycle, relationship with Him.

A child with its Father.

Security, identity, belonging.

Relationship before function.

We must know how precious and loved we are to embark on this school or we will become legalistic and harsh. We must know we are the beloved of God on whom His favour rests.

Because being favoured by Him can lead to life becoming a tad awkward...ask Mary...

She was described as *'highly favoured'*,[1] this resulted in her being unmarried with a baby on the way, culturally unacceptable to say the least...favour has its own interesting ways of working out...

You always know where you are with Him, but you never know what He's going to do.

He's always the same in who He is, but totally unpredictable in what He's going to do.

And He wants to develop a trust relationship with us.

So that we trust Him, and He in turn, can trust us.

Scary.

Both ways.

There's no stability in this place.

Control freaks may exit at this point.

But that's what it's all about.

Trust.

So if you've got that settled, you will always know what He's going to be like because He never, ever, changes the way He feels towards you but you'll never know what He's going to do.

I want to examine some more circles now, starting with the cycle of transformation.

In this one you will find yourself both stretched *and* out of your depth.

It is another 'd' word which is distinctly uncomfortable.

Development.

Development and distress go together in the cycle of transformation.

You want to shout, "Get me out of here I'm a Christian," but in your heart you know that this is Him and it is all for your profit – eventually.

If you respond properly.

Joyce Meyer describes it as being in a microwave oven, with God looking through the glass seeing you going round on the turntable as the heat gets higher, while you are shouting to be let out!

Very funny!

Provided that isn't your current experience.

Distress and development go together you need to understand this.

'Thou hast enlarged me when I was in distress,'[2] the psalmist says.

The psalmist is complaining about people around him; he's had enough you can tell and shouting for deliverance...

People are there to grow us in grace, the enemy is there to grow us spiritually – we mustn't confuse the two.

Everything can be turned to a profit.

There is nothing around your life right now that cannot be turned to profit.

So stop blaming people. What if God put them there for your benefit, growth, expansion and development?

What if?

"I wish," I can hear you say.

You can change the way you see them and the situation you know.

Make those choices.

Ask Him how He sees it...

That is the time when we are enlarged the most, if we change our minds.

When you are in distress is when God is developing something in you.

It's where He rebuilds your character and prepares you for what He has in store.

Development.

It most often follows a prophetic word where your name is in lights and you think stardom is just around the corner...

Ask Joe.

We've looked at him before.

Gets this word about leadership and next thing he knows he's down a pit and it didn't get any better but he ended up second only to Pharaoh...

God's ways again.

Can't odds it.

They surely aren't ours.

But so much better, the yield is so much higher; the future is so much brighter because He's bright, brilliant in fact.

His unchanging heart and His unchanging word to you becomes the place where you can stand in absolute confidence in the goodness of God towards you, regardless of your circumstances because He has something good planned for your future.

Jeremiah 29:11.

Feeling better?

It's not so bad after all is it?

Notes
1. Luke 1:28 NIV
2. Psalm 4:1 KJV

39 Feeling Or Faith

Sometimes God appears to withdraw.

One minute we are basking in His presence.

We can take the world on singlehanded.

The next, we are like Joseph, down a pit; darkness; misery, where did it all go?

It's part of the training.

What we are experiencing is Him moving us from feeling to faith.

You know about the three cats of course?

No?

Three cats walking along a wall: one in front called Fact, next one, Faith, and the third, Feeling.

All the time Faith kept his eyes on Fact he was all right. When He looked around at Feeling they both fell off the wall...

Moral – don't look at your feelings!

He gives us an experience of Himself and just as we are set to camp there, enjoying the experience asking, *"Shall we build three tabernacles?"*[1] like Peter on the mount of transfiguration; He moves the scenery and it all goes dark.

Very dark.

Now He wants us to learn to live not by feelings, the next meeting, the next conference, the next encounter, the next laying on of hands, but by faith.

Raw faith.

God says it; I believe it so that settles it.

'Faith...

...is the substance of things hoped for, the evidence of things not seen...'[2]

Uh huh...

Not so good.

The School of the Spirit

It is here we learn that the valley is the place where we grow, not the mountaintop.

We can't live on mountaintop experiences.

Ask Pete.

He wanted to camp there.

We have to have that most recent experience of Him taken away, so that He can give us something better, something more of Himself.

An absolutely cast iron certainty that He is as He says He is – whether we *feel* it or not.

Hope.

Steadfast and certain.

Whether the situation changes or not.

It doesn't matter.

We trust Him.

Forsaking

All

I

Trust

Him

F A I T H.

That testing time has to come.

After manifestation, comes hiddenness.

Sure as night follows day.

Ah.

Light first.

Followed by darkness.

He's done it before.

Now we see.

Perfect submission, all is at rest.

Lord, I trust you.

I don't understand, but I trust you.

He loves that.

Notes
1. Matthew 17:4
2. Hebrew 1:11 KJV

40 The Purpose Of Trials

'Don't think it strange when trials come.'[1]

Trials.

They are really important.

Not things to just go through but **grow** through.

That's what they are there for.

That you may grow.

Mature.

Lack nothing.

God is seeking to establish certain core character traits and values in you.

So that you rejoice in suffering.

And bless when you are persecuted and reproached, and evil is spoken of you.

You respond in the opposite spirit.

You don't give like for like.

"I know something about you too, pal!"

It's sometimes simply about learning the art of enduring under trial.

Some tests are over more quickly than others.

Maybe they are allowed, in order to teach you patience.

That's the purpose of trouble.

Tribulation works ....you fill it in.

Demonic oppression is there to teach you about power.

Human opposition teaches you grace.

Tension and difficulty teach you how to rest.

And trouble – well we know what that one is there for.

Endurance is a constant in this; you can't duck out or be rescued because you will have to go around that particular test again, until He is satisfied. He's saying, let Me grow these lovely attributes in you...stick with the process, you will be like My Son.

We never develop the character He wants to bestow upon us if we lose our grip on the maturity He is holding out to us.

Patient endurance under trial.

Wouldn't that be a place to come to instead of looking for the nearest fire exit?

"Endure hardness as a good soldier," [2] Paul says to Timothy.

Here we are with something else then.

Hardness.

No thank you!

But it's all part of the training.

Like fortitude.

We are an army.

In training.

Three steps here: training ground; proving ground and finally; battle ground...

Don't have time to get bored in this school, do you?

Stick with the programme.

We could be on manoeuvres tomorrow!

Notes
1. Matthew 17:4
2. Hebrew 1:11 KJV

41 Base Camp 2 – The Two Pathways

We talked about the purpose of trials.

Sometimes we need to stop and look at how far we have come and where we are headed.

Mountain climbing is not for the unprepared or ill equipped.

Patient endurance, perseverance and fortitude are keys.

Without them you will only climb a few hills in God, you'll never climb mountains.

Choices again.

'What man building a tower doesn't sit down and work out the cost?'[1] Quote of Jesus I think.

Time to slow down again and recap.

Beryl R Moore

Think really carefully about the next leg of the journey.

Take a look at what we have seen in this School.

It's not for the faint hearted.

Those with backbone not wish-bone.

God is gracious.

He won't love you any the less if you don't go on...

You always know where you are with Him but you never know what He is going to do next.

He's looking for maturity.

Doing things differently.

Out of step with others perhaps...

They won't understand from here on up.

Very few will walk with you and they won't say much.

Take stock beloved.

It isn't going to get any easier from here.

The atmosphere will thin.

Breathing will become difficult.

The School of the Spirit

You may sense the beginning of altitude sickness...

No disgrace.

He loves you just the same whether you stop now or go on.

Congratulations on getting this far.

Now you need His wisdom to respond to what He is teaching you and where He wants to take you.

He's turned you from enjoyment to endurance and the scenery has completely changed.

From church to kingdom.

Not many of those who started out with you are still there.

You can't cast out the cross and crucify the devil.

You have to embrace the cross and cast out the enemy of your soul.

Submit to God, *'you are My Friends if you do whatever I command you'*[2]

Suddenly we find we have moved around that circle to – friendship.

Here we find that there is no such thing as a casual friendship with God, no matter what people may say.

There are no **casual** friends in the Kingdom.

God is intentional.

He would like you to be the same, but He never forces you.

The work of God here in endurance is to produce, vulnerability and submission.

Surrender.

Not partial.

A place where you become so vulnerable you have no confidence in yourself at all.

Only in Him.

Then He will take your confidence in Him to a high place.

But it's that altitude thing again...

Are you really up for the next part of the climb?

Let's rest here a while, so you can think about the next stage of your journey where you will learn to communicate only with Him, with the Holy Spirit as your guide.

There are two pathways you see.

The road splits here.

The School of the Spirit

One is the pathway with lots of people, plenty of chat and interaction, doing things together...church.

The other is just – you and Him, walking into a life less ordinary – kingdom.

This path is overgrown.

You enter it on your knees.

And you only hear one voice.

The Holy Spirit.

Notes
1. Luke 14:28
2. John 15:14

42 Weakness

So the whole point of weakness is that He brings you to a place of vulnerability, insecurity and inadequacy.

"I can't..."

Perfect.

So far as He is concerned.

Uncomfortable.

For you.

Extremely.

Perfect for Him though.

He can move in.

He isn't going to make you strong, don't ask for it.

That needs to be settled.

He's never going to give you something that will keep you at a distance from Him.

He is going to **be** your strength.

Remember, He's going to **be** for you everything you need.

This is that.

Your insecurity and inability = his opportunity.

Nice one.

He's making you weak so that you develop submission, patience, dependence, perseverance, endurance, fortitude, faith, grace, mercy, humility, and gratitude...all those lovely things.

Oh my.

You become so grateful that you are no longer strong but weak.

No longer self-confident.

But leaning on the Beloved.

Now you sing with the joy of the Lord when you are in

difficulties, and you thank Him because you know He is right there with you in the midst of it all.

You know that for every problem there is provision.

So you wait confidently, "I know You, it's here somewhere, I'll just wait here until I see it."

You're confident.

You stop trying to escape.

And trade it for another 'e' word –

Embrace.

You embrace the cross with joy, knowing Christ is being formed in you.

You rejoice when you see your old man being killed off, you're no longer screaming to be delivered but jumping for joy at the relief of walking in the Spirit not in the flesh or your carnal nature.

You can really begin to say, "It is no longer I that lives, but Christ that lives in me."

And know this is increasingly the truth.

After the cross.

Resurrection life.

Beryl R Moore

Christ is formed in you.

Resurrection life springs forth from you.

Rivers of living water flow from you.

Refreshing others.

As you love them as He does.

See everything from His perspective.

Receive the wisdom that comes from above.

In this life.

Reigning over yourself and your circumstances, you put the enemy to flight.

Your name is known in hell.

Your flesh is under control

You are walking with the Lamb.

You're getting the hang of it, there is a place in God reserved for you that He wants you to have that will make others say you are so far out you'll never get back.

Indeed!

Absolutely right.

The School of the Spirit

This is the place of breakthrough and follow-through.

Living from heaven to earth not the other way around.

Now you don't have a breakthrough and lose it, but you have the strength to follow through.

Now you lead others in the same way you have gone, helping them to breakthrough and follow through.

There is a place here where the mysteries hidden in God are being revealed to you...

He calls you friend.

You call yourself His love slave.

The circle is nearly complete – this time round.

43 Pierce My Ear

Comes the time then, when you are so in love with Him that you ask if you can be His love slave, you ask Him to pierce your ear as the slave who loved the Master and didn't want to go free, and that you *'may dwell in the house of the Lord forever, and behold His beauty'.*[1]

Paul often described himself as a prisoner, or love slave of Jesus Christ.

It seems to relate to the power of the conversion experience.

For me, it was a complete turnaround, just like Paul – "I was like that, now I am like this".

'He who is forgiven much, loves much'.[2]

I so identified with this woman; still do.

I have no difficulty being His love slave.

But it isn't the same for everyone.

Many struggle with the steps we have already taken through sonship, servanthood, friendship and finally the one we are looking at now...

I know no easy answer, except to pray for the grace of yielding.

We do not know what rebels we are until we are asked to lay down our own plans and surrender to someone else, even if that someone else is the Lord Jesus Christ.

So how is it working out for you?

Have you enjoyed reading these sessions and made a mental assent, but know in your heart if He were to ask the ultimate of you, that you put your Isaac on the altar, you would not be able to part with him, or it, whatever constitutes your particular Isaac?

There is no shame my darling, no disgrace.

Though we call this a School, there are no exams to pass, no grades to win.

It is all an affair of the heart.

The Father is looking for a Bride for the Son.

One who will love Him.

The School of the Spirit

She is destined for the throne.

To reign and rule with Him for eternity.

Whatever you choose, you will reign and rule, but maybe not to the level you could have.

Decisions as we saw very early on, determine destiny.

Attitudes determine altitude.

He is not going to love you any the less.

But it isn't too late to put your whole self in…

Not just an arm or a leg.

It's never too late with Him…

He is the God of the second, third, and fourth, chance.

What happens is we run out of time.

If we procrastinate out of fear, we just run out of the time it will take Him to prepare us for the best He has for us.

But the choice is always yours.

No disgrace.

No shame.

No judgement.

Next we are going to look a little more closely at what God is aiming at…

See you then?

Notes
1. Psalm 27:4
2. Luke 7:47

44 Union

There are some who think that union with God is not possible in this life.

We aren't talking about something physical here, but deep calling to deep; spiritual union where two wills are united in common purpose and thought…

'I and My Father are One.'[1]

'I promised you to one Bridegroom…to Christ'.[2]

The moment we receive Jesus we receive all we need to live and enjoy the Christian life.

Jesus in us is the fullness of God.

We are in Him, He is in us, and He is in the Father.

Double wrapped.

The journey has just begun.

The journey to complete possession…

…His of you.

'I am my Beloved's and His desire is towards me…'[3]

So says the maiden at the end of the Song of Songs.

She has come on a journey into the heart of the Beloved.

She started out declaring she possessed Him –

'My Beloved is mine and I am His'…[4]

She ends, knowing she belongs to Him and no other.

She has dropped her claim to possess Him and allows Him to possess her completely.

No wonder we see the parallel of marriage so often in scripture – the two shall become one…

That is what God is after, that two shall become one.

You, melded into one, Him.

Where does He start and where do you end?

You have walked into the glory and been swallowed up in the brilliance.

No longer two lives to be lived, but one.

His.

Through you.

And you are more than content to have it so.

Someone asked Georgian Banov[5] what he was speaking on one evening and he was heard to say, "I don't know, I am a dead man."

No more opinions.

All is Him.

Seeing as He sees.

Speaking what He wants to say…

That sounds familiar… John 4:34.

Of course, that's what it is all about whilst we are here, doing what the Father wills. We say it, don't we? *'…on earth as it is in heaven'*.[6]

We must be about our Father's business, just the same as Jesus was and He wasn't referring to carpentry!

'Oh to be like Thee blessed Redeemer, this is my constant longing and prayer...' [7]

But there's only one way to do it.

Total consecration.

No longer two lives to be lived but one.

The anointing, the indwelling Presence, takes everything out of our hands...

So, question, how're you doing?

Questions you know are designed to transform your relationship and your walk with the Lord. A good teacher does their job best by questioning the pupils, making them think about what they really know and believe.

Questions are designed to transform your understanding of yourself and how you are changing on this journey of discovery.

It's not just about you understanding something more about Jesus.

You have to see yourself in a new way.

So how's it working out for you?

How do you see yourself now compared with when we started this journey?

How do you see and relate to Him now?

I'll leave you with that one...take your time.

Notes
1. John 10:30
2. 2 Corinthians 11:2
3. Song of Solomon 7:10 KJV
4. Song of Solomon 2:16
5. Bulgarian evangelist and songwriter lives in the USA.
6. Matthew 6:10
7. From the hymn by Thomas Obadiah Chisholm 1866-1960

45 The Anointing

In Pentecostal and Charismatic circles we hear much about *'the anointing'.*

It is something to be sought after and revered.

We don't go very far into John's gospel before we see what this is.

'The Son can do nothing of Himself'.[1]

"The works I do are not mine". (Paraphrase)

Union with God will mean we are prisoners of the Lord.

Just as Paul described himself.

No fame, glory, no reputation.

The anointing is the indwelling Presence.

We can do nothing unless He himself does it.

Helpless.

Useless.

Yielded.

We wait.

If He doesn't come and do it, it won't get done.

It's not a pleasant experience.

People are looking at you and to you...

Nothing happens.

Zilch.

Nada.

Nothing.

"Now would be a good time Lord..." dribbles off the end of your chin...

The loss of our natural strength, the self-life is a necessity; the anointing carries with it the absolute Lordship of Jesus Christ.

The School of the Spirit

All Him.

The way up is down.

He has a series of elegant tests that take us lower each time.

He must increase...

Self-serving must go.

You fear elevation knowing what is in you; the predisposition to taking something of the praise for yourself...

'For I know that in me dwelleth no good thing...' [2]

We say we love Him, but we like to have some input; our own way as well...

No condemnation.

Reality.

'I delight to do Your will O my God'. [3]

Little way to go yet.

He's finding us out.

But He knew already; it was us who didn't know ourselves.

He brings us into loving subjection to Himself.

This isn't you being squashed but Him being pre-eminent.

We take our worth from Him.

You come into everything He won on the cross by submission to the Divine will.

His Lordship over us, letting Him have the pre-eminence.

The Lordship of the Spirit is not something that strips us, takes everything from us or keeps us down so we dare not move. It frees us from the tyranny of the self-life.

The Lordship of the Spirit is to bring us into the fullness of His headship...*'of His fullness we have all received'.*[4]

Trouble is, bottom line, it's not someone else's fullness we want, but ours!

We want it ourselves, come on, 'fess up, you want to feature!

But the Holy Spirit cuts that ground from under our feet saying, "***In Him*** my darling, ***in Him*** dwells all the fullness of the Godhead bodily."

Outside of that...you know it, zilch, nada, nothing...

We can't actually enter this School until we see this; the altogether 'other-than-us' way, He is.

Back where we started I think...

He is utterly different from us.

'*You are from beneath, I am from above*' – key.[5]

That is the difference, this is where we clash, and this is where we learn to yield, submit, to the Higher Authority.

The cross is where His will and my will cross...

Very clever!

Takes a lifetime but we have to start somewhere.

'*Thy will be done*'[6] – that'll be it.

Notes
1. John 5:19
2. Romans 7:18
3. Psalm 40:8
4. John 1:16
5. John 8:23
6. Matthew 6:10

46 The Clash

So, we are discovering the clash of wills, the clash of judgements, the clash of purpose, the clash of minds, the clash of ideas, the clash of perceptions, the clash of values… clash, clash, clash…

He is altogether 'other than' us in the way He looks at situations, people, and circumstances.

Just look again at the Gospels, there was a clash between Jesus and the religious leaders, yes, but He also clashed with His disciples – frequently.

They thought one thing, He thought something completely different.

He has a heavenly mind.

We have an earthly one.

That's our journey right there.

The transformation mentioned in Romans 12:1-2.

Being transformed in our minds.

During the course of this journey you will find Him saying things that just don't compute to your natural mind.

Sometimes the 'other than' inside you is insisting on a certain course of action that you consider absolute madness!

But the insistence is there.

You cannot escape it.

It has to be this way or no way.

Do the thing.

There is no reconciliation here; that old, earthly man has got to allow the new heavenly man to take precedence.

'If anyone desires to come after Me, let him deny himself… and follow Me'[1] takes on a new meaning.

Deny yourself; your arguments; your justifications for why you can't do it; your assessment of the situation; your judgement; your suspicion; your common sense – deny it.

Do the thing.

Just as He tells you.

We can never be sure we are doing the right thing unless we submit to Him; keep Him in that place of pre-eminence; ourselves in that place of submission to His Lordship.

Rendering Him first position, and ourselves His love slaves.

He intends that we should have everything; He isn't second lining us, this is done to bring us into fullness, not deny us.

He must have His place of absolute Lordship in order that we come into His fullness.

We come after Him in order to derive all the benefits, all the value, He places on us.

We aren't being repressed or squashed, but following after.

Who minds taking second place, if you can get all that comes to the One in first place?

'Get in line Winifred.' [2]

It's the only safe place to be...

Notes
1. Matthew 16:24
2. The Jungle Book – classic Disney animation based on Rudyard Kipling's book.

47 Keep Waiting

We're nearly finished now, but we need to look at some examples of famous people who got the right idea but missed it when it came to timing.

They just didn't wait.

We've talked about the importance of this before.

You can hear God, but miss Him in terms of not waiting for His time, you know.

Saul is a classic of course, Samuel has said, *"Wait until I arrive,"* but to test Saul's obedience, he hangs about a bit: 1 Samuel 15:11 and following tells the story.

Saul fell victim to his own insecurities and was *'impelled'* to take precipitate action.

It lost him the throne.

223

Or take the case of King David; he wants to get the ark back to Jerusalem – his motive is right, his heart is right, his sense of God's purpose is right, but he got so enthusiastic, so carried away with his own ideas he forgot to follow the instructions on **how** it should be done...someone died as a result...and it was some time before the ark went back to where it belonged.

You can see this story in 2 Samuel 6.

What am I saying?

Keep in a place of prayer.

Make sure you know not only His intention but His timing.

Don't get the instruction and run off with it.

Keep checking.

Stay connected

He is the Head.

You are the body.

The body takes instructions from the head...

Wait for His timing.

Another place of the clash of the earthly with the heavenly!

How's it working out for you?

48 Keep Walking

'I walked a mile with Pleasure;

She chatted all the way;

But left me none the wiser

For all she had to say.

I walked a mile with Sorrow,

And ne'er a word said she;

But, oh! The things I learned from her,

When sorrow walked with me.' [1]

This Robert Browning poem came to me today as we

near the end of our time together.

I must leave you because from here on, it is His hand you need to hold, not mine.

My work was to introduce you to the Holy Spirit, get you engaging with Him and then be ready to be dismissed when the job was done.

When the friend of the Bridegroom hears the Bridegroom's voice, you see, it's time to hand over the bride... John 3:29.

I could teach you many more things about the School of the Spirit but I sense Him saying you need to walk with Him now.

You need to learn what it's like to walk with Him alone, you don't want other people's experiences, you want to be able to write your own book about your love journey and it's high and low places.

Jesus said He would send 'another' Comforter someone who was just like Him.

Interesting word 'another'.

'Another' just like Me, he was saying in John's gospel, *'and when He comes He will lead you into all truth and…will bring to your recollection everything I have said'.*[2]

Couldn't wish for more could we?

Someone who **is** Jesus, living inside us.

The School of the Spirit

Now your part is to walk with Him on your own.

Three's a crowd they say...

Our problem remains though, it's the same one Israel had when they refused Jehovah – we want a man, someone with skin on, to rule over us.

Why?

So we can argue – that's why.

If you don't believe me, have a word with Mo when you get there!

The people fought him every step of the way.

But you can't argue with God and win.

That's your problem now.

He's moved in.

Closer.

He's after intimacy.

Union in fact.

No longer someone with skin on, He's here in person...

If you fool yourself like Israel did and ask for a man to rule over you, you could end up with a Saul, just as they did.

The Lord said of them when He sent Samuel to them '...*they have not rejected you but they have rejected Me,'* 1 Samuel 8:7.

What an indictment.

God's chosen people.

Reject Him.

When push comes to shove – rejection is His portion.

Does He retaliate?

I think not '*Father forgive them, they know not what they do...'* [3]

Your turned back and stiffened neck; your desire to have maturity and have it now please, never elicit anything but love and forgiveness from Him.

He knows what rebels we all are.

And He loves us.

Without condition.

But He won't leave us there.

The least we can do is recognise our own wilful nature, our desire to be our own king and repent.

Have another thought.

Turn.

Return.

To the lover of our souls.

In order to be healed, we must first accept we have a terminal condition.

The leprosy of sin, self-government – clings to us.

But there's a cure!

1 John 1:9.

He is faithful.

'He has not dealt with us according to our sins...' Psalm 103:10.

Well that's a relief right there.

Notes
1. Robert Browning Hamilton *Along the Road*
2. John 14:13 and John 14:26
3. Luke 23:34 KJV

49 Holy Desire

I sense we are not quite finished.

'Still, still, without ceasing

I feel it increasing

This fervour of Holy desire

And often exclaim

Let me die in the flame

Of a love that can never expire!' [1]

A poem of Madame Guyon, martyr to the Holy Spirit, as she was described.

It's one I linger over and breathe out in prayer... **'let me die**

in the flame.'

The flame of Your love...

The fire burns for you, you see, not against you.

It's just that...

Sometimes doesn't feel like it.

But –

'His only design, your dross to consume and your gold to refine...' [2]

Death is conquered by life.

It's a slow process, step-by-step, choice after choice to go the way of the Spirit not the way of the flesh. But...

Fulcrum point is reached.

We tip over; the balance changes.

At last there is **'more of You and less of me'** until we can say **'all of You and none of me'**.[3]

When this point is reached you will unconsciously give help and assistance to everyone who crosses your path...

Jesus in you touches them.

His love for them flows through you.

'Greater works than these', of which He spoke in John 14:12 become a reality.

But you are aware of nothing but Him...you are **'gazing on the crucified'**...that's an old hymn –

'All for Jesus! All for Jesus

All my being's ransomed powers;

All my thoughts and words and doings,

All my days and all my hours...'

Sums up absolute surrender I'd say.

Right there...

'Let my hands perform His bidding;

Let my feet run in His ways;

Let mine eyes see Jesus only;

Let my lips speak forth His praise...

Since mine eyes were fixed on Jesus,

I've lost sight of all beside;

So enchained my spirit's vision,

Gazing on the Crucified...' [4]

That'll be it.

Notes

1. A W Tozer *The Christian Book of Mystical Verse* Martino Publishing CT USA 2010 p53
2. From the hymn probably written by Samuel Jarvis *How Firm a Foundation* 1762.
3. From the worship song *Lily of Valley* by David Ruis
4. From the hymn Mary D James *All for Jesus, All for Jesus.*

50 Ground Zero

'As many as are led by the Spirit of God, these are the sons of God' Romans 8:14 isn't referring to gifts.

It is referring to those who are **living** in the School of the Spirit, being taught by Him daily.

We started by saying His ways weren't our ways – Isaiah 55 – and during these few precious days together we have seen illustration after illustration of how He likes to do things and how He thinks...This is the Lord's doing...

Surely it is marvellous in our eyes!

But He's challenging us again.

To a, one on one, walk with Him alone.

Chips are down.

Face to face.

Heart to heart.

Will you have **Me**?

Here's My cup, will you come and drink?

To have and to hold, from this day forth, cleaving only to **Me**?

No matter how far we have gone, or think we have gone in our Christian walk, He presses this one thing, *'Have I been with you so long, and yet you have not known Me, Philip?'*[10]

It is in this place, ground zero; we find everything we **thought** we knew about Christ is brought into the light of His countenance.

Under His scrutiny…

Ground zero.

"That's where we need to start beloved," He says.

Right there, with your understanding of *Me*.

He did it all the time, with Nicodemus – a man of the law, he knew a thing or two…With the woman of Samaria, she thought she knew some things; the helpless cripple, 38 years in the same place, thought he knew what he needed; the man blind from birth; all started again from ground zero drinking from the well of water that would **never** run dry.

The School of the Spirit

'Without Me…' John 15:5

I know, don't rub it in, zilch, nada, nothing!

He will not touch the thing until it is beyond all human hope.

He's not healing the old man; He's making a new one.

After His image.

'I Am the bread of life'…[11] there is nothing here in this world that can feed you, nothing in this world that can meet your need…

Bread from heaven or we are dead.

Life in the Spirit

*'Let My people go that they might worship **Me**'*[12] Exodus 7:16

He demanded of Pharaoh.

Not let them go so that they are free to roam, but that they might worship **Me**.

He has to always bring us back to Himself.

'Lord, to whom shall we go? You have the words of eternal life…'[13]

So, what Pharaoh is holding you back from worshipping Him alone right now?

What Isaac do you still need to put on the altar?

Questions, questions...

Make you think though don't they...

God bless you.

Notes
1. John 14:9
2. John 3:35
3. Exodus 7:16 NIV
4. John 6:68

Meet the Author

Beryl Moore is first and foremost: spiritually – a passionate lover of God and naturally – a mother and a grandmother.

Passionate about the Kingdom of God, as her lifestyle and teaching reflects, she believes every Christian can and should hear God for themselves.

She majors on teaching prophecy, spiritual warfare and leadership with an emphasis on the need to return to a God-centred lifestyle, by restoring the Creator/creature relationship to its proper place of honour, respect and intimacy.

Reading extensively, with an interest in the early church fathers and mystics such as Julian of Norwich, Madam Guyon, Teresa of Avila and Bernard of Clairveaux, and more recent prophets including A. W. Tozer and Graham Cooke, Beryl's work reflects her desire for the Kingdom to come in the lives of her audience.

Currently her main role involves raising up leaders, warriors and champions through training, consultancy and mentoring; with a particular emphasis on training leaders.

Beryl R Moore

She lives in a small village in Kent where she works alongside the leader of a local church assisting in building a strong community of believers who focus on living a Kingdom lifestyle and bringing heaven to earth.

Originally called into the deliverance and healing ministry her focus changed ten years ago from 'hands-on' ministry to imparting knowledge to others. She is both eager and willing to share everything she knows to anyone who is interested.

With a love for God and His word, Beryl's philosophy is what she gently refers to as 'replacement theology' the renewal of our minds as we abide in the place Jesus died to give us, namely Himself. She teaches extensively on the need to abide, stay, dwell and remain where God the Father has placed us, in His Son. Her heart's desire is that all God's people know and experience the outrageous love of God.

We hope you have been inspired and renewed in your journey through *The School of the Spirit* devotional. For details of more of Beryl's teaching material, downloads and You Tube videos visit our website at www.sovereignministries.co.uk

New book coming soon from Beryl Moore *Thy Kingdom Come* 365 daily readings about her journey through the sermon on the mount.